Finding Ourselves In The Great Stories Of The Bible

Cycle B Sermons for Advent, Christmas, and Epiphany Based on the Gospel Lessons

Mark Ellingsen

CSS Publishing Company, Inc.
Lima, Ohio

FINDING OURSELVES IN THE GREAT STORIES OF THE BIBLE

Library of Congress Cataloging-in-Publication Data:

Names: Ellingsen, Mark, 1949- author.
Title: Finding ourselves in the great stories of the Bible : Cycle B
  Sermons for Advent, Christmas, and epiphany based on the gospel lessons
  / Mark Ellingsen.
Description: First edition. | Lima, Ohio : CSS Publishing Company, Inc.,
  [2023]
Identifiers: LCCN 2023015221 (print) | LCCN 2023015222 (ebook) | ISBN
  9780788030789 | ISBN 9780788030796
Subjects: LCSH: Bible stories, English. | Bible. Gospels--Criticism,
  interpretation, etc.
Classification: LCC BS550.3 .E55 2023 (print) | LCC BS550.3 (ebook) | DDC
  252/.61--dc23/eng/20230726
LC record available at https://lccn.loc.gov/2023015221
LC ebook record available at https://lccn.loc.gov/2023015222

For more information about CSS Publishing Company resources, visit our website at www.csspub.com, email us at csr@csspub.com, or call (800) 241-4056.

e-book:
ISBN-13: 978-0-7880-3079-6
ISBN-10: 0-7880-3079-5

ISBN-13: 978-0-7880-3078-9
ISBN-10: 0-7880-3078-7

Contents

Foreword

The church is in a mess in America as 2023 comes to a close and the new year begins. We have not made much progress in slowing down the growth of the "nones" (religiously unaffiliated). Many of our congregations are still paying the price for the closing down of live worship during the pandemic. We may never get some worshippers back in the building, and very few church leaders want to come clean with the truth that worship online does not nurture faith like live worship does.[1] Meanwhile church leadership and the local, Conference/District/Synod level are still doing "business as usual." No sense of urgency about the need to get moving as the baby boomers slow down and whose passing away will drastically diminish membership rolls and clergy ranks (unless the millennials find Jesus in middle age).

What will it take to turn things around? I've already written a book to answer this question. We need a strategy which will force the Church away from its strategy of trying to make faith relevant by reinterpreting it in light of the latest fad or the trendiest worldview. Rather, what the Church needs to do is to become more interesting, more counter-cultural. We need to offer the world something none of the cultural gurus or the market provides. That entails becoming more biblically literate, being overtaken by the biblical stories, seeing ourselves as living them out in daily life. What could be more odd or intriguing to twenty-first-century Americans than people who orient themselves by a first-century (and older) book, who act like commitments matter, fairness counts, and that wealth, power, health, or prestige don't matter as much as spiritual realities?[2]

If you agree with my analysis then you will also agree that we need more preaching which reflects this approach, more sermons about the great stories of the Bible, but which try to get congregants to find themselves in these stories, to discover new things about themselves in the accounts. That is what this book is offering. The lectionary for Sundays in Advent, Christmas, and Epiphany offers great stories for the flock. But they are so familiar. How can you get fresh sermons out of them? We freshen up these stories when we do what Martin Luther, Augustine, and other great homileticians did, tell them in such a way that we get our congregants to find themselves in these stories.[3] What follows are some sermons which endeavor to put into practice what I am preaching about, what we'll need to do to stop all the undesirable trends in church and society I've been lamenting here. Like I've written in all the sermon books I have done, I urge that you make these sermons your own, don't just use them verbatim. Be sure you preach them in such a way that you are locating yourself and the needs of your flock in the framework of the biblical stories and ideas I offer. Preaching is a team sport (involving preacher, congregants, theological resources, the Holy Spirit, and our Lord). But every team needs its own playbook, even if you are running similar formations as other preachers. I'm just giving you my playbook (some formations, strategies, or musical scales to use) in what follows, but you implement/experience the Bible's stories for yourself.

Speaking of team sports, over the years my sermons and even the ones in this book have been the result of the work of a team. The congregations I've served, students in my classes, and especially the lady I live with have always had input in my thinking (along with the giants of the faith I can never escape). But for this book, the main conversation partner, as in the case of all my other books, is my special friend through half a century of happily sharing in a marriage (and a few years of friendship and love before that). Happy golden anniversary, Betsey!

NOTES
1. Nicholas Carr, *The Shallows: What the Internet Is Doing To Our Brains* (New York and London: W. W. Norton, 2011), esp. p.194; see my article "Social Media and the Costs of Distraction," *Journal of Interdisciplinary Studies* , Vol.XXXIII, No.1/2 (2021): 541-542.
2. Mark Ellingsen, *Ever Hear of Feuerbach? That's Why American and European Christianity are in Such a Funk!* (Eugene, OR: Cascade, 2020).
3. I explain how to construct sermons like this in my *The Integrity of Biblical Narrative: Story in Theology and Proclamation* (Minneapolis: Fortress, 1990); Mark Ellingsen, *Lectionary Preaching Workbook,* Series IX Series, Cycles B,C,A (3 vols.; Lima, OH: CSS, 2012-2013).

The End Is The Beginning; And The Beginning Is The End

It seemed to have happened during Jesus' final trip to Jerusalem, after the Palm Sunday event. The end (the end of Jesus' life) was just beginning. And what happened in that final visit to the temple in Jerusalem? At the beginning of this new chapter in Jesus' life, the start of his final days, at the time of new beginnings in the lives of those like us who followed him, in the midst of the controversies which were all around him, Jesus talked about the end! He prophesied the destruction of Jerusalem (13:1-2). He foretold what would happen to his followers, seemed to be predicting the end of the age. And then he issued a famous warning:

> Beware, keep alert; for you do not know when the time will come. It is like a man going on a journey, when he leaves home and puts his slaves in charge, each with his work and commands the doorkeeper to be on the watch. Therefore, keep awake — for you do not know when the master of the hour will come, in the evening, or at midnight, or at cockcrow, or at dawn, or else he may find you asleep when he comes suddenly. And what I say to you I say to all; Keep awake (vv.33-37).

Keep awake. This gospel lesson, the words of Jesus, were all about the end times — about the Second Coming. He was telling the disciples and us to be prepared and alert, to be prepared for his coming. The timing of God and Jesus here is important. They want us to consider the end times as the dawn of a new beginning. There's a lesson for that message today. It has to do with Advent. This story has a lot to teach us about Advent and also about new beginnings in life.

There's a real tension here. I'd call it a creative tension. Here we are at the beginning of the church year. You knew that the church year begins in Advent, right? Here we are, the First Sunday in Advent, the very first Sunday of the church year, and the church picks Bible lessons that talk about the end times. (After all, it's not just our Gospel Lesson; our Second Lesson for today also talks about the end [1 Corinthians 1:8].) No, here we are at a new beginning, and there's a lot of talk about the end. Oh, but that's the way God and the church see it. End and beginning, beginning and end, belong together. In God's plan of things, the end is the beginning. But on account of sin, the beginning is the end.

It may sound trite to you. But it is God's way to make new beginnings out of ends, and because of our sin, to bring to an end someday the new beginnings that have just begun. With God, all beginnings are endings; and all endings can be good, new, and beautiful beginnings. That's God's style. A quote commonly attributed to the Latin philosopher Seneca, a contemporary of Jesus, is on target; "Every new beginning comes from some other beginning's end."

The season of Advent reminds us that we'll see God more clearly, that life will be a little sweeter, if we just get in harmony with God's way of doing business. With God, on account of our sin, the beginning is the end. But the end is the beginning.

This is the way God works. That is also the way of the world since sin entered our world. Now God has always been making new beginning out of ends, always making something out of nothing. That is how he created the world. He made the world, is still making the world out of what its ultimate end is — out of nothing.

Of course we know that the beginning of time, that perfect world God first created, did not last. Our sin brought it to an end. But God took that ending and brought a new beginning out of it. He sent Jesus to make the world new, to give us new life. With God, the end is the beginning. But because of sin, the beginning is the end.

Think of it: In the midst of the chaos of sin, God brought about a new beginning in the world. He gave the people of Israel, he gave us, the Law, the Ten Commandments. But this new beginning had an end. With Jesus, the commandments have come to an end, just as need for the temple in Jerusalem to offer sacrifices to God came to end with the Roman destruction of Jerusalem. (Jesus seemed to prophesy that in our gospel lesson today.) No need to offer sacrifices to God any longer, as Jesus has done it all for us. The new beginning that God created after the fall into sin has come to an end in Jesus.

Yes, with new beginnings there are always ends. Commandments and temple sacrifices are at an end. They no longer save. Jesus' life, his saving work, is the new beginning which puts an end to the old ways to get saved. Jesus' birth, life, death, and resurrection are the beginning of something new for you and me! But this beginning is also an end, the ultimate end. Because while on earth all our beginnings will have endings, that's why you need to keep awake so you don't miss that something new is on the horizon. Yes, everything will end on this side of the grave, for only God's love endures forever. The Bible sings that song everywhere.

This word is certainly present in our first lesson from the book of Isaiah (64:1-9). This lesson was written at a time of great disappointment for the people of Israel. About fifty years before this lesson was written thousands of Israelites had been carried off into captivity, away from their native land, after being captured by the Babylonian Empire. Then almost fifty years later these Hebrew exiles had been permitted to return to their homeland, to start rebuilding Jerusalem (which had been destroyed earlier by the Babylonians).

Anyway, to make a long story short, the Jews returned. It seemed such a hopeful time, the end of the exile and the beginning of a new era. But then the new beginning came to an end; sin, pride, and sloth got in the way of the Jews' efforts at rebuilding Jerusalem. They were failing in their efforts to return Israel to its former prowess. They started rebuilding Yahweh's temple in Jerusalem, but they had not succeeded. Yes, all the great hope of their new beginning were fading away into a disappointing end. In this First Lesson, the prophet says it all:

> We all fade like a leaf, and our iniquities
> like the wind, take us away (Isaiah 64:6b).

We all fade like a leaf. On this side of the Second Coming, because of sin, nothing lasts forever.

Every new beginning has an ending. The great French philosopher Jean-Paul Sartre wrote about the "fragility of being," how readily it can cease to be so that it is no longer.[1] Physicists describe in their Second Law of Thermodynamics that in every system the entropy (the amount of unfocused energy in a system) will never decrease. We are all gradually decomposing or dying with each passing moment.

Saint Paul once said it is profoundly in his letter to the Philippians. In the third chapter of that epistle (v.7) he told us about what a Christian is to make of life. The message was: Don't make anything finite count for your good. Don't let it count too much. It's all passing away. Our earthly beginnings have an end. Don't let them get in the way of eternal things. Beginnings always have an end.

Oh, but this is not the whole story of our Bible lessons on this First Sunday in Advent. Our gospel and the other lessons proclaim a word of hope too. God takes endings and makes new and glorious beginnings out of them. So get ready, and don't miss the new things God has in mind for you.

Back to our gospel lesson: During the last week of Jesus' life, as he challenged the old establishment in Jerusalem that was withering away with Roman occupation and would eventually be destroyed, our Lord knew death was near. He knew that he, his followers, and eventually his fellow Jews would suffer. The end was near. And yet with death in view, with the destruction of Jerusalem as it had been since the temple had been rebuilt, Jesus gave his followers like us hope. He dreamed of a better day when he would come again in glory. The end that he and his followers were facing would be the doorway to one of God's great and glorious new beginnings (the most important in all human history)! In life it's true that the beginning is often an end. But for God the end is the beginning, the beginning of new blessings he gives us.

This same word of hope is present in our First Lesson too. It is a word of hope for you and me. Put yourself in the shoes of the Hebrews who had returned from Babylon. Yes, there was a lot of disappointment among us, a lot of doubt about this God of ours (Isaiah 64:6-7). The new beginning in Jerusalem was not all we had expected. In fact it was starting to feel like a dead end. But the prophet (probably not the historical Isaiah himself) still dreamed of a new beginning in the midst of that despair. He prophesied that God would come again to be with his people, not count their sin and claim all his people, making them new (vv.1-3,8-9). Out of Israel's and our own latest tragic ending, God comes to give a new beginning.

This is the way our God makes new wonderful beginnings out of the tragic endings we encounter in life. I don't care if it's the death of a loved one, a broken marriage, a stifled career, a bad reputation in school, or on the job. It doesn't matter. God is always there to give you a new beginning, a fresh start out of the tragic mess you and I have put ourselves into. In life, because of sin, the beginning may be the end. In fact, every beginning in life has to have an end. But we have a God who makes good and hopeful beginnings out of ends. The end is the beginning with God. Keep that in mind the next time tragedy strikes or what's been good doesn't feel quite as good anymore.

Yes, there is a wonderful symmetry in the church's celebration of Advent for this Sunday: The end is the beginning, even if the beginning is the end. Our worship service on this first Sunday in Advent has two messages for us. Don't get too hung up on the wrong things. Don't put your priorities in the wrong place. Every one of our brand new projects, even some of God's projects, are passing away. They're finite. They'll all have an end. Only God and his word endures. When you live with that insight, then you are getting ready to welcome Christ into your life. Advent is about preparing to welcome Christ. Start it this week.

Oh, but this is not the whole story. The beginning may be the end. But with God, the end is just the beginning. We have a God who is out to restore us, to give a new, good, and fresh start. No matter how tragic an end you've come to in your life, God did not want that for you. But he has something good planned for you. Yes, with God the end is surely the promise of a new fresh beginning. Jesus' word in our lesson was that what feels like an end is the beginning of the end times, when he would conquer on the cross or come again. He wants you and me to know that right now, since that first Christmas, we have been living in the beginning of the end of time!

What a great God we have. Life is always full of endings, even the things we love must end. But in Advent now we are reminded that we have a God who wants us to be prepared, because he is always there to give you and me a fresh start. The beginning may be the end most times. But at the altar (receiving The Lord's Supper) and in all your disappointments in life you are going to meet a God who makes fresh beginnings out of ends. The beginning is the end in life, but with God the end is the beginning.

I love how the famed German Christian martyr Dietrich Bonhoeffer (he lost his life trying to put an end to the Hitler regime) once put it in an Advent sermon. He was talking like Jesus did, saying these words to us:

Lift up your heads, you army of the afflicted, the humbled, the discouraged, you defeated army with bowed heads. The battle is not lost, the victory is yours — take courage, be strong! There is no room here for shaking your heads and doubting, because Christ is coming.[2]

Take heart and heads up. With God, all our ends will have a new beginning, and even at the end of time, Christ's *return* will forever make things new. Keep alert this Advent. It's time for getting you ready for Christ to come, to put an end to what is wrong by giving us all a fresh start.

NOTES
1. Jean-Paul Sartre, *Being and Nothingness*, trans. Hazel Barnes (New York: Washington Square Press, 1969), pp.40-41.
2. Dietrich Bonhoeffer, "Come, O Rescuer," in Geffrey B Kelly and F. Burton Nelson, eds., *A Testament To Freedom: The Essential Writings of Dietrich Bonhoeffer* (New York: Harper San Francisco, 1990), p.237.

Getting Ready For Christmas

Those of us living in the Judean countryside in the first century sure had our opinions about that preacher John. There was no middle ground about how to take that man. Many of us regarded him as an odd-ball, as a religious fanatic. Running around with camel's hair cloak. The man can't even get a decent meal for himself, eating nothing but locusts and wild honey (v.6). And all that talk of his about repentance and baptism is troubling (vv.4,5). Why, that's the way those crazy Hebrews from over by the Dead Sea operated. Essenes you call them. They were just a cult. Why this John sounds like one of them.[1]

There were others of us who saw in John a holy man, maybe even a prophet, a true prophet! John's attire was reminiscent of what Elijah often reportedly wore (2 Kings 1:8). And it was taught among the Hebrews that Elijah's return would be a sign of the end of the age (Malachi 4:5). Could John be Elijah come again? Was this man a forerunner of the end times, of our liberation from Roman occupation of our land? His nomadic lifestyle, his living in the wilderness, was suggestive of the way Moses and the faithful lived when on the Exodus and deliverance from slavery by God. Yes, for some of us, hanging around John connected us with a real man of God; with someone who really could put us in touch with God's final plans for us!

With followers like those of us who admired the man, some of us probably thought of him as someone who could lead us and deliver us. But John would have none of that veneration. He told us not to focus on him, because the one coming after him is the one with power. John modestly said that he wasn't even worthy to stoop down and tie the shoes of the one who was coming, the one whom John was talking about (v.7). The one who was to come would not just baptize with water like John had, but baptize with the Holy Spirit (v.8).

Mark got it right in citing today's First Lesson from Isaiah (40:3) to claim that John came to prepare the way for Jesus (v.3). And it is true that John did urge his hearers to focus on the one coming (Jesus), not on himself (v.7). In making this point, John got his followers and got us away from the material distractions of the moment. John did not want his hearers to be so caught up in who he was and what he was doing, so caught up in the political realities of the day that they misinterpreted what his message was all about. It's so easy for us with Christmas on the horizon to get caught up on all materialism now associated with it (the latest gifts and must-have trinkets), that we wind up misinterpreting the Christmas message, make it just a day for family and more goods. (After all, that's why a lot of congregations today don't worship on Christmas Day — because it's all about family [and enjoying the presents], we say). Maybe John's shunning of fancy clothing and his refusal to indulge in the latest sumptuous foods (v.6) should be taken as a reminder to us as we prepare for Christmas that the holiday is not all about the finest things money can buy.

Yes, this is great advice for preparing for Christmas. Just two more weeks to get the shopping done, right? After all, this is what Christmas is all about for most Americans. Only two years ago, with the scepter of the pandemic still around, total holiday sales reached $886.7 billion dollars! And the average American family spent $1,463.[2] Americans don't have their priorities right. Maybe that's why the American Psychological Association found some years ago that 38% of Americans believe their stress level increases during the holidays.[3] No, even if we have already purchased all the Christmas presents by Thanksgiving (the latest trend the business and media gurus have conned us into obeying), we are not really ready for Christmas, since we've gotten our eyes off the real prize — Jesus and his coming into our lives.

John the Baptist did not make that mistake. He came as the one who would get Israel, and now get the world ready for Jesus' coming. See how John deflected everyone's interests on the material distractions to Jesus' coming. That way Israel and we could be better prepared for him to come, better prepared for Jesus.

"Be prepared." The Boy Scout motto has a point. "All things be ready, if our minds be so," William Shakespeare once wrote.[4] John the Baptist and our faith say that Jesus is coming, that Jesus is ready, so it is good you are ready too (v.7).

Good preparation helps you enjoy the moment. Think how much more relaxed you are at the Christmas meal you prepared if all the most important preparation was completed earlier in the day, how much easier and enjoyable the days before Christmas can be when you already have the presents.

When you are not prepared for what comes next, not yearning, it seems that our brains stagnate, and we miss out on a lot of the pleasures that come with preparation. Neurobiologists tell us that preparation (and spirituality) feels good. This is a function of experiencing the feel-good chemicals of the brain (dopamine, serotonin, and oxytocin) which are secreted when the brain's prefrontal cortex is activated. And when involved in preparation and faith, that is the part of your brain that goes into overdrive. Preparation and faith in Jesus feel good, are rewarding.

Here is the catch: Because dopamine is a drug to which you can build up a tolerance, once planning ends and has become reality, we gradually experience less pleasure from what is the cause, become less happy if we are not planning another project to get more dopamine.[5] Get it?

If you want to get more excited about Jesus, enjoy Christmas a little more, find new, fresh ways to get ready for Jesus and Christmas. In secular America today, maybe all it would take is for a family deliberately to spend more time talking about Jesus and his birth than Santa Claus and the must-have presents.

How to prepare for Jesus' birth and his coming? Back to John the Baptist. John the Baptist gives us a model, at least Martin Luther thought so. Recall that John focused his attention on Jesus' Coming, repentance, forgiveness of sin, and a baptism of repentance (vv.3-4,7-8). Luther put it this way:

> This then is the preparation of Christ's way and John's proper office. He is to humble all the world and proclaim that they are all sinners. This is truly to humiliate man, to cut out and annihilate his presumption. Aye, this is indeed the way to prepare the way of the Lord, to give room and to make way.[6]

Christmas is not about you and me, but about Jesus. We need to wake up! The famous modern theologian Karl Barth talked about preparation as waking up. He wrote:

> Christians... are those who waken up... as they awake they look up, and rise, thus making the counter-movement to the

downward drag of their sinfully slothful being. They are those who waken up, however, because they are awakened. They are roused, and they are thus caused to get up and sit in this counter-movement.[7]

Note the work of the Holy Spirit in waking us up, in preparing us. You and I don't do it. We can't get ourselves ready for Jesus to come. No, you and I need the Holy Spirit to get us ready for Christmas. So if you find yourself thinking of Jesus in the next week or two, amidst all the hustle and bustle of getting ready for Christmas, pinch yourself and stop. Because then you're going to be on holy ground. Those magical moments when you get ready for Christmas the right way are miracles! The Spirit is present in those moments.

Need more insights about how wonderful these moments of right preparation for Christmas can be? Don't forget John the Baptist's words today that the Christ to come will baptize with the Holy Spirit (v.8). When the Holy Spirit comes, he does not come alone. He comes with Christ (Galatians 4:6; 2 Peter 1:11). God himself gets you and me ready for Christmas, for his presence.

In fact, Christmas is not just a once-a-year thing. Christ is already present in your life! You would not be here right now if he was not present in your life. When you believe that (and remember faith is a gift), it opens you to be prepared for the future. That's what being prepared is all about, being ready for the future, anticipating how good it is going to be because you are ready for it. Think with me now about how inviting the future is when Christ is always with us like he has been over the years with us. And so the future is not something to fear. It's a little familiar, because Jesus, the one who has been guiding you will be there. Famed New Testament scholar of the last century Rudolf Bultmann nicely explained how hopeful we Christians can be about the future because John the Baptist and more importantly Jesus have prepared us for it:

> Therefore, this hope or this faith may be called readiness for the unknown future that God will give. In brief, it means to be open to God's future in the face of death and darkness.[8]

Because Jesus has been with us over the years, we are ready for this Christmas 2023 when you and I will meet him again. We are also ready for the upcoming new year and all the years up ahead. And that confidence that comes with being prepared because you can see Jesus' presence throughout your life, that insight leads us to realize with Martin Luther King Jr. that "tomorrow is today."[9] It's urgent that you and I get ready, get ready for Jesus in our lives and all the Christmases to come, because what we do today affects tomorrow. But we can proceed with the confidence Rudolf Bultmann talked about, with the course Dr. King showed in his life. You can face the future with all its turmoil and death with confidence, because we know the Jesus who is coming now will be with you and me in the future too.

Yes, Christmas is almost here. There is even less time until the next opportunity you have to meet Jesus in your life, because though the Spirit's always showing up with him, too often you and I are not prepared and we miss him. Just like all the Christmas trappings are already in the stores, so Jesus already has your and my future lined up because he's already in our lives through the Holy Spirit. Heads-up that you don't miss him again. Our loving God in Jesus will be in the events of your everyday life this week (like he always is) to get us up, so we see him and are changed by him! And the more you keep that in mind, the more you find yourself in John the Baptist's message, the more prepared you'll be for Christmas, for life, and for the future. Praise God for John the Baptist, and how getting into his story gets us ready for Jesus, so that your life and mine can be filled with Jesus and be prepared for what comes next. Oh it's so good to have a season like Advent to get us prepared for all this.

NOTES

1. These themes are reflected in The Dead Sea Scrolls, IVQ.14
2. For these statistics, see J. Graig Shearmanm, "NRF Says 2021 Holiday Sales Grew 14.1 Percent to Record $886.7 Billion," (January 14, 2022) at press@nrf.com; 2021 Deloitte holiday retain survey, "Holiday shopping: Establishing the next normal," *Deloitte Insights* (October, 2021), at www2.deloitte.com/content/dom.insights,articles/US$164630_2021-holiday-retail-survey.
3. Statistics reported by David Levine, "Why Are the Holidays So Stressful?" *U.S. News* (Dec. 7, 2018), at https://health.us.news.com/wellness/mind/articles/2018-12-07/why-are-holidays-stressful.
4. William Shakespeare, "Henry V" (1599).
5. See Stefan Klein, *The Science of Happiness*, trans. Stephen Lehmann (Cambridge, MA: DaCapo, 2006).
6. Martin Luther, "The Witness and Confession of John the Baptist," *The Complete Sermons of Martin Luther*, Vol.1/1, ed. John N. Lenker (Grand Raspids, MI: Baker, 2000), p.124.
7. Karl Barth, *Church Dogmatics*, Vol.III/4, eds. G. W. Bromiley and F. F. Torrance (Edinburgh: T. & T. Clark, 1961), p.581.
8. Rudolf Bultmann, *Jesus Christ and Mythology* (New York: Charles Scribner's Sons, 1958), p.31.
9. Martin Luther King Jr., "Our God Is Marching On!" (March 23, 1965).

Advent 3
John 1:6-8, 19-28

To Live As A Prophet!

We have another version of the story of John the Baptist this week. He may not be portrayed by John in quite as strange a way as he was last week in Mark's gospel. But put yourself in the shoes of the priests and Levites (assistants to the temple priests in biblical times) living in the first century. The Bible says we priests and Levites have been sent by those Pharisees who were committed to keeping the faith pure (v.19). What do you make of this nomadic preacher, John? He's obviously getting a lot of attention in the countryside. We're suspicious of him. Why, the masses seem to be taken in by this guy. We religious and political authorities have to do something to stop this guy, before he marshals the masses. Who knows what happens next once he gets people to follow him in all this foolishness? Once that happens, good order will be undermined, and who knows what happens next. We're no friends of Roman occupation, but starting a revolution against them like those Zealots and maybe this John advocate will be suicide.

This is the background for challenges the priests and Levites issued to John. In last week's sermon we noticed how some things John did, according to Mark's gospel, suggested to the masses that he might be Elijah reincarnated, a sign of the end times. And with all that talk of John about the end times and maybe threatening the established order might make him seem to some as the long-awaited Messiah come to set Israel free. These ideas would make John even more dangerous, if he got people believing this. So in hopes they could put him on the spot, that John would make such outlandish claims about himself, the priests and Levites asked him point blank who he was. John said point blank that he was not the anointed one (*Christos* in the Greek language) (v.19).

Then his establishment critics asked him if he was really Elijah and he denied that too (v.21a). They were trying to get John to show himself a disloyal Hebrew, a cultic leader who rejected what was sacred in the traditions of Israel in order to undermine his clout with the masses. The strategy was not working. They tried another way, to see if John would say he was a prophet, somebody on the level of Isaiah or Jeremiah. And John said "no" to that one too (v.21b).

Well let's unpack that one. Wasn't John the Baptist a prophet? Yes, but not in the way the Jews thought of prophets, not in the way the world thinks of prophets today. John teaches us what a prophetic life today is all about. As Martin Luther once put it on a sermon on this text: "Therefore, in the simplest and most straightforward manner, he [John] denied being a prophet, although abounding in all the qualities of a prophet."[1] And he's inviting you and me into that way of life. He wants a church full of prophets — a nation full of prophets (Jesus' prophets). Let's break it down now, to see how we can avoid being prophets like the one John the Baptist did not want to be, but be prophets like John himself was. God wants us to be, has made us prophets like John.

Of course in the eyes of the world, like the world in which John himself lived, prophets were/are seen as crazy. Be honest, now, when you get away from the Bible, aren't prophets weird? David Koresh, the leader of the Branch Davidian cult which engaged in an infamous mass suicide thirty years ago in Texas was a prophet. The founder of the Mormon Church Joseph Smith who had *The Book of Mormon* revealed to him was a prophet. Sun Myung Moon of the Unification Church is a prophet. Prophets are crazy. It's like the famed nineteenth-century British female author George Eliot (just her pen name) once wrote : "Among all forms of mistake, prophecy is the most gratuitous."[2] Italian novelist and philosopher Umberto Eco was no less critical of prophecy as he observed that we "fear prophets and those prepared to die for the truth, for as a rule they make many others die with them, often before them, at times instead of them."[3] No wonder John the Baptist did not want to be confused with being one. How can this pastor of yours then go on to say like in the sermon title that God wants us to be prophets?

The Protestant Reformer John Calvin had a nice way of explaining biblical prophecy in a more palatable manner. He wrote:

> By the term prophecy, however, I do not understand the gift of foretelling the future, but as I Corinthians 14:3; the science of interpreting *scripture*, so that a prophet is an interpreter of the will of God.[4]

Calvin makes clear here that prophecy has nothing to do with crazy ecstatic experiences, is not about claiming "what the Spirit told me (in my private experience)." It's not about foretelling the future on the basis of your reason or intuition. No, prophecy is nothing more than interpreting scripture accurately, reporting what the word of God has to say about the will of God. No, to be a prophet, a true prophet, does not involve sacrificing your mind. Isn't that what John the Baptist was doing in his prophecy of Jesus and whom he would be, just interpreting scripture? Notice how he cites scripture (Isaiah 40:3) in his prophecy in our story from John (v.23). This kind of biblical authorization for John's prophecy appears in all the first three (synoptic) gospels (Matthew 3:3; Mark 1:2-3; Luke 3:4-6).

Real prophets aren't crazy after all. But in the eyes of the world, they do some crazy things. They may take on the establishment, challenge illicit authority, speak out at work when someone is getting the shaft for the wrong reasons, identify incorrect behavior for what it is (a sin), name the name of Jesus or testify to God when the secular context they're in discourages such rhetoric.

Yes, prophets are Christians who do crazy things. Some of the craziest things they do is get themselves out of the way, even when they've gotten a lot of attention for themselves because of the bold stances they've been taking. Can you better understand now why the priests and Levites and the Pharisees did not like John? They were the authorities (in the case of Pharisees recognized as the holiest of Hebrews). John the Baptist was stealing attention from them, and then not acting like they did after he got the crowd's acclaim. Martin Luther had a nice way of making this point. He claimed that John the Baptist directs people away from himself to Christ.[5] Elsewhere in the gospel of John, it is said of John that he was a "burning and shining lamp" (5:35), but not the light.

We are called to live like John the Baptist, to devote our lives to seeking the will of God, getting out of the way and away from the acclaim, so it is clear that like John our witness is always to Jesus and only to him. This way of living gives a wonderful testimony to the fact that we are not saved by who we are, but by Christ and him alone. Martin Luther also makes a profound point on this matter. In a sermon he proclaimed:

> It is, therefore, important that we learn from the example of John the Baptist to preserve this testimony concerning Christ. For the moment this insistence and doctrine are gone, people begin to preach human works...[6]

Too much attention to piety and your spiritual renown leads to a compromise of grace.

Four and one-half centuries after Luther there was another Martin Luther who preached a similar sermon about the dangers of leaders paying too much attention to themselves and their power. In a 1968 sermon at his home church in Atlanta, Dr. King spoke out against leaders with a "drum-major instinct." Everybody likes to be praised, he noted, wants to lead the parade. But Jesus gave us a new norm of greatness; he said (and its reflected in John the Baptist, I say) that greatness comes in service.[7]

Introducing Dr. King leads us to realize that prophets also have a word with political implications. John the Baptist himself gave offense to some in the Jewish establishment of his day. His entire ministry was without official authorization. Should not Christians walking in his shoes be challenging the economic establishment which marginalizes African Americans, Latinos', and women? We all know about the wage gaps, the income gaps, the health-care gap, and the real estate redlining which victimizes these minorities in comparison to white men. Shouldn't our denomination and our congregation start trying to do more about these issues? Isn't it time we lived prophetically to the point that the establishment gets uncomfortable with us, like the priests and Levites tried to trip up John? Until the powers that be in this town, in this state, begin to worry more about our church and denomination, we're not doing John's prophetic thing. It's like Martin Luther King wrote in his book *Stride Toward Freedom*:

> Any discussion of the role of the Christian minister today must ultimately emphasize the need for prophecy. Not every minister can be a prophet, but some must be prepared for the ordeals of this high calling *and be* willing to suffer courageously for righteousness.[8]

What Dr. King wrote here about clergy, he's saying it about all who would stand with John the Baptist, including laity in the room.

I'll say it again, though: Being a prophet involves getting yourself out of the way to highlight Jesus. And so it's not a glamorous job.

It really is like the nineteenth-century American humorist Josh Billings once said: "Don't ever prophesy [he said]; for if you prophesy wrong, nobody will forget it; and if you prophecy right, nobody will remember it."

Nobody will remember your true prophecy if you are getting out of the way. No. there's no glory for the prophet in prophecy. All the glory there is belongs to God.

Has the John the Baptist story moved you, made you want to be a prophet like him — condemning sin, pointing to Jesus and justice, getting yourself out of the way? This is what Christians do. The world may say we're crazy, but that's what Christians are designed to do. (If the world's not saying that, we're not doing Jesus' and John's thing.) But there's a rich benefit in living this way, so compelling as we approach Christmas. I'm talking about the wonderful intimacy with Jesus that's related to prophetic living. The original Martin Luther explains this experience so compellingly. He once proclaimed in a sermon:

> Therefore, this gospel deals with the great article about Jesus Christ, that we should receive *him*, kiss and embrace him, cling to *him*, never allow ourselves to be torn from *him* nor *him* from us. This is the chief article of Christian doctrine and on it rests our salvation. When one possesses this central truth, good works will then follow immediately...[9]

When we're doing prophecy, we spend a lot of time getting kissed and embraced by the one who is coming. You become someone who cares more about him, about justice, about right and wrong, than you do about self-promotion. To heck with what the world says!

NOTES

1. Martin Luther, "The Witness and Confession of John the Baptist," *The Complete Sermons of Martin Luther*, Vol.1/1, ed. John N. Lenker (Grand Rapids, MI: Baker, 2000), p.122.
2. George Eliot, *Middlemarch, A Study of Provincial Life* (London: William Blackwood, 1871-1872).
3. Umberto Eco, *The Name of the Rose* (San Francisco: Harper Collins, 1994).
4. John Calvin, *Commentary On the First Epistle of Paul To the Thessalonians*(1539), in *Calvin's Commentaries*, Vol.XXI, trans. William Pringle (Grand Rapids, MI: Baker, 2005). p.299.
5. Luther, "The Witness and Confession of John the Baptist," p.122.
6. Martin Luther, "Fourth Sunday in Advent — First Sermon," (1532), *The Complete Sermons of Martin Luther*, Vol.5, ed. John N. Lenker (Grand Rapids, MI: Baker, 2000), p.82.
7. Martin Luther King Jr., "The Drum Major Instinct" (1968), in *A Testament of Hope: The Essential Writings of Martin Luther King, Jr.*, ed. James Washington (San Francisco: Harper & Row, 1986), pp.260,265.
8. Martin Luther King Jr., *Stride toward Freedom* (1958), in *A Testament of Hope*, p.481.
9. Luther, "Fourth Sunday in Advent," p.82.

Advent 4
Luke 1:26-38

Our Brother, Our Soul-Mate, Jesus Is Coming!

It was the sixth month of Elizabeth's (the mother of John the Baptist) pregnancy (v.26), so it could have been maybe in the year 7 BC.[1] God sent the angel Gabriel to Nazareth in Galilee to reveal exciting news to a virgin named Mary. Luke reports that she was engaged to a member of the line of King David, Joseph (v.27). You know the story, but use your imagination to experience it with Mary.

The angel appeared, greeted her as God's "favored one" (v.28). How would you have felt to encounter an angel? Of course she was perplexed, scared, and wondered what made her favored (v.29). God's messenger (that's what angels are — messengers — it's the meaning of the Greek word *angelos*) tried to calm her down, assuring her that she had found favor with God (v. 30). (The Greek word here literally translates "grace." Mary would receive a special blessing or love from God.)

Gabriel went on and began to describe to Mary how she would conceive and bear a son who would be named Jesus. (The name Jesus was the common form of the name Joshua, and we all know the biblical Joshua's role in saving God's people at the Battle of Jericho.) She was told this son of hers would be called Son of the Most High, and he would be given David's throne, reigning over the house of Jacob forever as King (vv. 32-33). Hard to believe had you been there, right?

Mary asked how it all could happen. She was a virgin after all. The angel told her how the Holy Spirit would make it happen (vv. 34-35). And then Mary was told to visit her kin Elizabeth, learning that she would have a son (John the Baptist) who would remove all barriers, "For nothing is impossible with God" (vv. 36-37). And hard to take all this in, Mary said, "Here I am, the Lord's servant, let it be with me according to your word." (v. 38). Wow! What faith. What a great story. God is so good and loving to give us this gift of himself. But Mary's faith is so compelling. Don't you love her? Almost love her like a mom, the mom of our faith. Hold on to that point, because in a way she is.

Great story, but what does it mean for everyday life, with Christmas just around the corner? Let's start with the main gift—with what this story says about Jesus. Now recall that the name of Jesus is related to the Hebrew Joshua — its Greek version. Jesus would be a kind of Joshua. In Hebrew, the name means "Savior" or "Yahweh saves!" (Keep that in mind the next time you call his name.) Mary and we learn a lot about Jesus from the Annunciation of his birth in our lesson today. We learn also that he is both Savior and Son of God (v. 35). As we penetrate further into the birth we are celebrating this week, the importance of it all for everyday life will become a little clearer.

The Protestant Reformer John Calvin sets the stage for these insights. He praised the Incarnation, the knowledge that God has taken on flesh like ours. He claimed that this gives us confidence. He put it this way:

> This gives us good reason for growing confidence, that we may venture more freely to call God our Father, because *his* only Son, in order that we might have a Father in common with *him* who chose to be our *brother*.[2]

Do you follow the logic of this point? It entails that Jesus Christ is our brother! The Incarnation, Christmas, means that Jesus is *your* brother. Not just some distant historical figure of the past. He's your brother. And likewise, God is not some distant deity. He's family — a father of our brother Jesus, as such our father too. The founder of Methodism John Wesley put it this way. He said that Jesus is "the common head of mankind, a second general parent and representative of the whole human race." Wesley calls Jesus the "well-beloved Son."[3]

What does it mean to see Jesus as a brother, as kin who represents you and me? As siblings, does that entail that we share a common mother? Martin Luther said there is a sense in which this is true. As he once put it:

> We see here how Christ, as it were, takes our birth from us and absorbs it in *his birth*, and grants us *his*, that in it we might become pure and holy, as if it were our own, so that every Christian may rejoice and glory in Christ's *birth* as much as if he had himself been born of Mary as was Christ... O, this is the great joy of which the angel speaks. This is

the comfort and exceeding goodness of God that, if a man believes this, he can boast of the treasure that Mary is his rightful mother, Christ his *brother*, and God his Father.[4]

We are celebrating a family birthday, not just Jesus', but also our own births (our own spiritual births) this week.

Jesus is family. His celebration is ours. What does all this mean for everyday life? Again Luther provides thoughtful observations on this matter (in the same sermon about the Incarnation that I've been citing). He says that if Christ is our brother, his birth ours, then any idea that you have to do something to be saved is absurd! We are already children of God, since we are kin of Jesus. As he was born in purity, so you and I are now (re)born purely, since his birth is our birth.[5]

To these ideas Luther added:

> If Christ has now thus become your own, and you have by such faith been cleansed through *him* and have received your inheritance without any personal merit, but alone through the love of God *who* gives to you as your own the treasure and work of *his* Son...[6]

This sort of intimacy with Jesus leads to pleasure. Brain scientists are finding from brain scans that religious experiences of this sort of intimacy lead to the secretion of good-feeling brain dope.[7] What's the pay-off of Jesus coming into our soulmate? Think about this biological insight. Don't you feel good and secure in the company of your family? Well when you know Jesus as your brother and soulmate, that's how your life can start feeling, whenever you get swallowed up in the Christmas story and the story of the Annunciation to your mom. Come to think of it, maybe this is why the thought of Christmas does make people feel good and secure.

This sort of intimacy with Jesus follows from all we share with him. Martin Luther nicely captures this intimacy in one of his sermons. We talked about that last week, how Luther wants us to kiss and embrace, and cling to Jesus.[8] Think about Jesus your soulmate that way the next time you're in prayer, or even as you think of him now or read the Bible or see the Christmas decorations.

One of the great saints of the Catholic Church, Bernard of Clairvaux (you know of the loving dog named after him), was a mystic who thought about our relationship with Jesus this way too, he is recorded as stating:

Such conformity [of the soul and the Word of God] joins the soul in marriage to *the* Word ... it has become *his* bride... When loves comes into the soul it changes everything else into itself and takes the affections captive. The soul therefore that loves, loves, and knows nothing else... They are bride and Bridegroom... But this Bridegroom, remember, is not only loving; *he* is *love himself.*[9]

Love in a good marriage changes you. This is Bernard's point. Since our partner is now love himself, no wonder partnering with Jesus changes us. His love takes control of faithful people who are in love with Jesus, part of his family. That means love is in control, all your affections and feelings are under control of that love. Life is a lot different when you're part of Jesus' family.

Christmas is almost here! Jesus is coming! Our very own brother, the one with whom we share the salvation he won for us, is coming. Be sure to celebrate! His birth is the birth and joy and salvation for us all. And it feels so good. This week, be sure you don't forget in the midst of the Christmas hustle and bustle to hang out with your soulmate. He'll always be around, this week and in the weeks to come. Get ready to celebrate his birth. It's a kind of birthday for you and me too. So sweet to have such a loving soulmate and his faithful mom.

NOTES

1. This comment presupposes that Jesus was likely born in 6 BC. This is based on accounts of his birth in the gospels with reference to Herod's reign who died in 4 BC and was obviously alive when Jesus was born (Matthew 2:2) and also the fact that Jesus is said to have begun preaching at about thirty years of age (Luke 3:23 in the fifteenth year of the reign of Tiberius Caesar (Luke 3:1-2.) Many scholars calculate March 25 in 7 BC or later as the date of birth of John the Baptist. This would make Mary's pregnancy to begin in December with a late August birth in 6 BC.

2. John Calvin, *Commentary On a Harmony of the Evangelists, Matthew, Mark, and Luke* (1553), in *Calvin's Commentaries*, Vol.XVI/1, trans. William Pringle (Grand Rapids, MI: Baker, 2005), p. 43.

3. John Wesley, *Sermons, V,* in *The Works of John Wesley,* Vol.5 (Grand Rapids: Baker, 1995), p. 55

4. Martin Luther, "The Birth of Jesus," *The Complete Sermons of Martin Luther,* Vol.1/1, ed. John N. Lenker (Grand Rapids, MI: Baker, 2000), p. 144.

5. *Ibid.*

6. *Ibid.,* p.145.

7. Andrew Newberg and Mark Robert Waldman, *How God Changes Your Brain: Breakthrough Finding From a Leading Neuroscientist* (New York: Ballantine, 2010), esp. pp.55-56,159.

8. Martin Luther, "Fourth Sunday in Advent — First Sermon," (1532), *The Complete Sermons of Martin Luther,* Vol.5, ed. John N. Lenker (Grand Rapids, MI: Baker, 2000), p.82.

9. Bernard of Clairvaux, *Sermons on Song of Songs,* in *Varieties of Mystic Experience,* ed. Elmer O'Brien (New York: Mentor Books, 1965), p.103.

Living The Christmas Story

Come along with Jesus' family on the trip to Bethlehem. You know the story. It was not their hometown (Nazareth), though Joseph had family ties there through his ancestor King David. Seems that the Roman Emperor Augustus had demanded a census throughout the empire, and everyone needed to go to their ancestral home for the registration.

By the way, questions have been raised if the census actually transpired, since Quirius who is noted in the account was not the governor of Syria during Herod's reign. It is also unlikely that spouses would have had to travel with their husbands unless they owned property in Bethlehem through their side of the family. Be that as it may, let's tell the story.

Nazareth and Bethlehem are ninety miles apart. Think of travelling ninety miles on foot or horseback with a pregnant wife. Oh, it was just flatland walking and riding near the Jordan River. But think how long it would take. A good week, and longer with a pregnant wife, because ten miles was absolutely the best you could expect to cover.

If it was winter when the holy couple travelled (and we can't be sure about the precise time of Jesus' birth, especially given how many Christian churches do not accept December 25 as his birthday), the temperature would likely have been in the thirties. And no matter what time of year, they would have endured rain. The paths often led through forests where lions and bears resided. Travelers had to be alert, and Mary was likely in no condition to run much had they been attacked.[1]

Bandits or robbers were also common hazards along trade routes like the one Mary and Joseph took. Solitary travelers were better off joining trade caravans for protection. We don't know for sure whether they availed themselves of this protection, or made the dangerous trip on their own.

Well, after an ordeal like that, Mary and Joseph arrived in Bethlehem, and we are told that Mary delivered Jesus (v. 6). Where? In what circumstances? Could Jesus have been born in the streets? You wonder, since we learn that there was no place for them to stay in a town inn, and that the baby Jesus was wrapped in cloth and laid in a manger (v.7). So maybe the old story of him being born in a stable is a report of where the birth actually transpired.

Giving birth in ancient times, before the advent of hospitals and skilled obstetricians, was a risky, dangerous undertaking. The death rate for mothers was quite high. Maybe Mary and Joseph found an experienced and wise midwife. But no matter, Mary (and indirectly Joseph) had gone through a harrowing, though joyful experience. Mothers in the congregation, imagine what Mary had been through. Delivery in ancient circumstances, after a long trip, and away from home!

We want the very best for our children and grandchildren. That's why we wanted all those must-have gifts for them, why we want luxury and beautiful things for ourselves. Mary, Joseph, and their child (the king of the universe) received none of those things. All those Christmas trinkets and material blessings seem pretty empty in light of the fact that God did not think that the holy family, that his own Son, needed them.

Ever wonder about those folks with homes in Bethlehem? And how about those who no doubt had big rooms and had gotten a room in the inn? They probably didn't need all the spaciousness they had. And here Mary was pregnant. Had just delivered a baby! How could anyone have been so heartless as not to have given up or shared a room with a new mother and her newborn? Martin Luther raises this question so powerfully and poignantly in one of his Christmas sermons. As he said it so well:

> There are many of you in this congregation who think to yourselves, "If only I had been there! How quick I would have been to help the baby! I would have washed his linen... Yes, you would! You say that because you know how great Christ is, but had you been there at that time you would have done no better than the people of Bethlehem. Childish and silly thoughts are these! Why don't you do it now? You have Christ in your neighbor. You ought to serve him, for what you do to your neighbor in need you do to the Lord Christ *himself*.[2]

Luther's right. The fact that there are street people in our town and metropolitan area, families not even sure of a having a Christmas meal, or at least not eating heartily like most of us will, is testimony to how often you and I shut the door on Jesus when he and his family come for shelter. No, we shut the door on Jesus all the time.

The mad quest for wealth is the governing reality of life for all of us. The shepherds in the fields did not have good jobs. They were practicing a largely despised occupation at the time, and so were pretty much nobodies in their society. Yet they are the ones to whom God revealed his Son, the Savior, even sending angels to sing to them. (The fact that the shepherds shared King David's pre-monarch vocation [1 Samuel 16:11] also seems relevant in God's plan to reveal Jesus to them, a way of linking Jesus to the Davidic heritage.) How amazing that it is those who are poor and outcaste who first come to know Jesus. "The last shall be first..." (Matthew 20:16)

A Pew Foundation poll taken before the pandemic found that 59% of African Americans claimed religion is very important in their lives compared to 40% of the total American population.[3] Those considered on the outside are more faithful. And that seems to extend to poverty too. A 2021 Gallup International poll found that in countries surveyed, respondents in the lowest income bracket were about 17% more religious than those in the highest.[4] Think of the church growth in less developed nations, while we in America and the West lose numbers.[5] We need to be reminded that it is the poor and outcast, those who are outside the establishment, who are the people God uses.

Listen to the angels' song, as Martin Luther tells it. They sing of peace and goodwill (v.14). Peace and goodwill for those tortured about their worth. Not only do they promise peace to those of us tortured or down on our luck in life, but the peace they promise in their song diverts us from evil's domination of the earth.[6] John Calvin said much the same thing one time:

> When men hear this single *word* [the mercy of God], that God is reconciled to them, it not only raises up those who have fallen down, but restores those who were ruined, and recalls them from death to life.[7]

God indicates in the story of Christmas that he paid no attention at all to what the world is or has. Nothing matters if you don't have Christ. Mary and Joseph as well as the shepherds may not have had any material blessings, not even a roof over their heads for the holy family. No, those in their fine houses or rented rooms in Bethlehem that night had it a lot better. But we are still remembering Mary and Joseph as well as the shepherds today. Whoever heard the names of those hard-hearted Bethlehemites! Who needs the things of the world, not even all those must-have Christmas gifts? They won't last long. Not like the things and people who belong to Jesus.

To these points, Martin Luther added other insights about living the Christmas story. If we can believe this story, he says, we could never harm another human being. For how could we harm or hate someone with a body like the one God has (remember he took on human flesh)?[8] This is an insight into the angels' hymn about peace on earth and goodwill among all (v.14). But it is also a wonderful affirmation of who you and I are as human beings. The human body, your body, is good enough for God. He mixed the divine essence with a body like yours. How's that for a word of self-respect and self-worth? Don't be so tough on yourself anymore. The human body, your very own body, is good enough for God.

With Jesus and you sharing that body of yours, a body you share with all human beings, the Incarnation and Christmas are reminders that we share much in common at Christmas, that it is a festival that reminds us we are not alone in life. That's why it's appropriate that Christmas is also a family day. Anglo-American novelist Taylor Caldwell once commented on Christmas in this light. In a confession of its meaning for her she wrote: "I am not alone at all... I was never alone... We are never alone. Not when the night is darkest, the wind coldest, the world seemingly indifferent."[9] Christmas reminds us that no matter how bad and lonely things are, because evil does not dominate the world, we are all sharing the very body God took on, he himself dwells in a body like ours.

Getting yourself wrapped up in the Christmas story has other implications for everyday life. Let's consider what the encounter with Jesus did to the shepherds. They did not abandon their jobs and take up religious occupations. Though called by the angels and responding to their call, they still went back to their jobs, but no doubt changed. Knowing like us that they were not alone, they were probably from then on committed to serving God in their jobs. Encounters with Jesus (Christmas) change you. You become someone who can't help but seek to do good. When you see the baby Jesus in the manger, it changes you like hanging around any baby changes you. Only this baby makes an even bigger change. Again Martin Luther preached it so well:

> Our dear Lord Christ is responsible for creating a heart and soul with a new and different mind, will, delight, and love. The result is that whereas a man previously was only interested in earning money and acquiring property, now having come to a knowledge of Christ, he would not only sacrifice money or property but also his body and life before he would deny Christ and *his word*.[10]

By the end of this week, we'll need to leave the Christmas story to get back to everyday twenty-first-century life. But it doesn't work that way for Christians. We can't really leave the Christmas story. We need to live in that story in order to receive the affirmations we all need of self-worth, need it in our struggles with despair as it reminds us how valuable we are to God. What God did for us at Christmas leads to a life of service and love for others, an appreciation of the poor and the "nobodies" in our community. American President Calvin Coolidge had it right: "Christmas is not a time nor a season, but a state of mind. To cherish peace and goodwill, to be plenteous in mercy, is to have the real spirit of Christmas."[11] God's love for you and me, the story of Jesus, can keep that spirit alive in you come next month — next year — the rest of your life! It comes from living the Christmas story.

NOTES

1. See n.1 of Advent 4 for more details on historical speculations about the actual birth of Jesus. Eastern Orthodox churches continue to celebrate Christmas on the date used by the earliest Christians, January 6.

2. Martin Luther, "Nativity," in *The Martin Luther Christmas Book*, trans. Roland Bainton (Philadelphia: Fortress Press, 1968), p.38.

3. Pew Foundation, "Survey" Black Americans attend church and pray more often," (2020), at https://apnews.com/article/black-americans-attend-chruch-pray-more-be5b10abc-863c0975c11a92a488e67a3.

4. WIN-Gallup International Global Index of Religiosity and Atheism (2012).

5. See n.2 of Foreword for a source with which to obtain statistics.

6. Martin Luther, "Holy Christmas Day — Second Sermon," (1534), *The Complete Sermons of Martin Luther*, Vol.5, ed. John N. Lenker (Grand Rapids, MI: Baker, 2000), p.111.

7. John Calvin, *Commentary On a Harmony of the Evangelists, Matthew, Mark, and Luke* (1553), in *Calvin's Commentaries*, Vol.XVI/1, trans. William Pringle (Grand Rapids, MI: Baker, 2005). p.115.

8. Luther, "Holy Christmas Day," p.113.

9. Taylor Caldwell, *Family Circle*, Dec. 24, 1961.

10. Martin Luther, "Holy Christmas Day — Sixth Sermon," (1534), *The Complete Sermons of Martin Luther*, Vol.5, ed. John N. Lenker (Grand Rapids, MI: Baker, 2000), p.149.

11. Calvin Coolidge, "Presidential Message," December 25, 1927.

Getting Reacquainted With Our Talkative, Creative, Caring God

John tells a different version of the Christmas story. He doesn't start with Jesus in the manger or with the journey of Mary and Joseph to Bethlehem. We don't even hear anything about the angels or the shepherds. No, instead we hear about what God was doing in eternity and what Jesus' divine nature, the Word of God, was doing before anything existed. You know this version:

> In the beginning was the Word and the Word was with God and the Word was God. He was in the beginning with God. All things came into being through *him*, and without *him* not one thing came into being. What has come into being in *him* was life, and the light was the light of all people. *(vv.1-4)*

Next John proceeds to refer briefly to John the Baptist who, though not the light, came to testify to the light (that is, to the Word of God who is the light) (vv. 6-9). Next we get a brief story of what would happen to the Word in the world, how its creator comes and the world does not acknowledge him, but those who receive him become children of God (vv.10-13). And finally comes the Christian story: We learn that "the Word became flesh, lived among us, and [that] we have seen his glory, the glory as of a Father's only Son, full of grace and truth" (v.14).

Usually the version of the Christmas story we repeat focuses on the baby Jesus. Today with John, we focus more on the story from God's side, what it teaches us about God and who he is. It's so appropriate to John that we use Christmas as a time to get to know God in his majesty, because the author of the gospel of John himself says the main point of the gospel is to appreciate Jesus' divinity, the fact that he is Son of God (20:31).

Okay, if Christmas is about God, what do we learn about our Lord? Well, from the beginning we find that he is talkative. In eternity, before there was time, he had a word who was always talking. God the Father was never alone; he always with a word (v.1). We have a talkative God!

Now we know that the words we speak authentically are who we are. When it comes to God, that's the sense in which the Word of God is God. Do you better understand now how Father and Son can be one, kind of like your words are distinct from who you are but are still you (of your essence)? Martin Luther put it this way one time:

> Therefore the world knows that nothing represents the condition of the heart so perfectly and so positively as the words of the mouth, just as though the heart were in the word... Thus it is also with God. His Word is so much like *himself*, that the godhead is wholly in it, and *he who* has the Word has the whole godhead.[1]

In fact, Luther goes on the say that the Trinity is like an internal conversation in God. In another sermon he put it this way:

> Thus, this Word has a true divine nature from the Father... No, this Word remains in the Father forever. Thus these are two distinct persons: *he who* speaks and the *word* that is spoken, that is, the Father and the Son. Here, however, we find the third person following these two, namely the *one who* hears both the *speaker* and the spoken *word*. For it stands to reason that there must also be a *listener* where a speaker and a word are found. But all this speaking being spoken and listening takes place within the divine nature and also remains there where no creature is or can be. All three — Speaker, Word, and Hearer — must be God *himself*...[2]

The Father is the speaker, the Son what is spoken (the Word), and the Holy Spirit in the listener. But they are all one. God sure is a talkative God. Is this not a profound, fresh way to understand the Trinity?

John tells us that God uses his Word to get things done. Human words are powerful things. Suppose I tell you to "stop," — pay attention. Aren't I likely to provoke some action? Well if human words can do that, think of what God's word can do. That's why it makes sense to say that God's word created the universe. Words are creative. I say "I love you, we are friends," and a relationship can be created. If our words can create, it's easier to understand how God's Word is creative. All God has to do is speak, and it gets things done.

It seems that God is also artistic. He is always looking to create good and beautiful things (vv.3-4). John 3:16 tells us God's motive in making the world, in speaking the word who is Jesus, is all about love. Yes, our God is a talkative, creative, and also a caring God. Think of the gift of Jesus at Christmas that way. Indeed God has been talking throughout history, even before history and the cosmos began (v.1). It's his talking that keeps the world in existence (kind of like a lack of talk in a relationship spells the end of that relationship).

God keeps the conversation going. Been that way throughout history, for as long as there has been God he's had a Word and a listener. (The Trinity teaches us that the Father has never been without the Son and the Spirit.) And this conversation is a rich one. Good conversations have that character. They open doors to new things. That's why the Word of God is always creating. The first-century Roman philosopher Seneca put it this way: "Conversation has a kind of charm about it, an insidious something that elicits secrets just like love or liquor."[3]

Human conversation is so magical, so mystical, and pleasurable. Keep that magic in mind today/tomorrow as you engage in conversation with family and friends. And then imagine how much richer, how much more magical and charming a conversation with God is. The conversation among Father, Son, and Holy Spirit opens new doors and is creative. Imagine how exciting it is when we get to share in that conversation! This is a creative word that overcomes darkness and chaos, a light that overcomes evil (vv.4-5,12-14)!

Our lesson and the Christmas story are all about the fact that this Word of God who has become Incarnate in Jesus is full of grace (love) and truth (vv.14,16). God has given us Jesus to communicate that word to us, to draw us into conversation with him. This is a creative conversation, God using it to make something new. It's a conversation with God that overcomes death and all the darkness that surrounds us. The darkness of loneliness that surrounds so many in America.[4] The darkness of poverty and racism which plagues so many Americans. Conversations with God can change that, make sure that you're no longer alone, no longer without, no longer regarded as a nobody. Conversation with our talkative God gives you companionship, gives you resources, gives us a sense that you're somebody. The light of a conversation with God removes all that darkness.

This is the meaning of the Christmas lights. This word, this conversation God has with himself, now includes you and me. That's why the Word became flesh, why Jesus was born. The Word living among us draws you and me into this creative conversation, and that means that we become part of God's creative process of making us and society better. Christmas is a time for making things better, for caring about the whole creation. And you and I can keep that Christmas celebration going as long as we get engaged with God's Word and get involved in God's conversation with himself.

One more thing about God and Christmas: It is a joyful time for good fellowship and conversation. Well, that's not surprising, because there's often a lot of good conversation at the family gatherings. Just like we Christians are celebrating God's good conversation when we say the Word became flesh. It seems that psychologists have found that the happiest people get engaged in twice as many substantive conversations a day as their less happy peers.[5] No wonder Christmas is a happy family time. It's filled with good, often in-depth conversation and reminiscences. And it is also no wonder Christians are happier people. And we do poll as happier quite significantly in comparison to the general public.[6] We get to sit in on God's conversation when we come to behold the Word of God lying in the manger, when we read the Bible, or every Sunday hear God's Word. We can have it prayer too. Why we Christians have a chance to be engaged in the divine conversation all the time!

Christmas is the opportunity to join and share in the joys, creativity, and fun of the conversation that God has been having with himself forever. It's there for you, here every Sunday, every time you open that Bible, talk about faith with someone else, or pray. Who says Christmas is just a one-day celebration. The Christmas party, the fellowship, and the joy of conversation are gifts God is giving us forever. That talkative God of ours is never without a word for us, never without his creativity, compassion, and love for you and me. Come join him in conversation now as we worship the Word in the manger. But don't miss all the other stimulating conversations waiting for you in the new year ahead!

NOTES

1. Martin Luther, Holy Christmas Day — Sixth Sermon," (1534), *The Complete Sermons of Martin Luther*, Vol.1/1, ed. John N. Lenker (Grand Rapids, MI: Baker, 2000), p.179.
2. Martin Luther, *Dr. Martin Luther's Exposition of the Fourteenth, Fifteenth, and Sixteenth Chapters of the Gospel of John* (1537-1538), in *Luther's Works*, Vol.24, ed. Jaroslav Pelikan (St. Louis: Concordia, 1961), pp.364-365.
3. Seneca, *Letters from a Stoic*, trans. Robin Campbell (New York: Penguin, 2004).
4. A 2020 Cigna poll found nearly 3 in 5 Americans feel lonely.
5. Matthias Mehl, Simine Vvzier, and Shanon Holleran, " Eaves-dropping on Happiness: Well-Being Is Related to Having Less Small Talk and More Substantive Conversations," *Psychological Science* 21, No.4 (April 2010): 539-541.
6. According to a 2018 Pew Research poll reported by Michelle Darrisaw, "It Turns out, Regular Church-Goers Are Happier, a New Pew Study Finds," (Feb, 28, 2019), at https://www.oprahdaily.com/life/health/a26251703/religion-happiness-pew-study/, in the US 36% of the actively religious describe themselves as very happy compared with only 25% of the inactively religious or religiously unaffiliated.

The Beginning Is Nothing: It's The End That God Counts!

As the first-born son of his family, Jesus was a big deal, the heir of the family. And so as was the custom in ancient Israel his parents brought him to Jerusalem to present him to the Lord in the Jerusalem temple. He was to be consecrated, designated as holy to the Lord. Also in accord with Leviticus 12, Mary was presented for a purification and a sacrifice of turtledoves, and young pigeons were offered (since the family obviously could not afford a sheep to sacrifice [vv.22-24]).

The Bible tells us that there was a community pillar at the temple door that day — a true man of God, Simeon. He was righteous and devout, a real believer. A good, faithful Jew. He was the kind of senior citizen everybody in the community respected. He was a man you thought the world of and he was not fanatic or nobody's fool. He was just a deeply religious, highly moral, wise man. He was a man who combined his deep faith with a social consciousness, with a concern about his nation's future and a hope that someday God would set Israel free again. As usual, that day, this community pillar went to the temple to pray (v.25).

Then there was another community pillar at the temple that day. She was elderly, like Simeon. Indeed she was probably older than he was. And she was deeply religious. The Bible says she was a prophetess, and remember since the Old Testament era prophets were people who were highly respected in the community — the educated upper class you might say. Saint Luke tells us that she was in the Jerusalem temple almost every day, praying and worshiping. She even did a lot of fasting (vv.36-38). Yes, Simeon and Anna weren't just community pillars. They were deeply religious. They had the kind of faith that was an inspiration to everyone who knew them.

Yes, these deeply faithful community pillars were in the Jerusalem temple that very day when Jesus and Mary came for the rites of dedication and purification. (Jesus had already been circumcised.) When it was time for him to be dedicated, that's when Simeon and Anna saw him. First, Simeon saw Jesus! That faithful community pillar had been chafing under the domination of Israel by the Roman Empire. The Bible says he had been longing for the Messiah, longing for God's especially appointed leader who would start a Jewish revolution against the Romans, a revolution that would set Israel free. He believed, old man that he was, that he would not have to die until he saw the Messiah (vv. 25b-26).

And then Simeon saw Jesus! He grabbed the baby in his arms and began singing a song that Catholics and Eastern Orthodox Christians sing at every celebration of the Lord's Supper to this day. (Lutherans used to as well.) It's called the Nunc Dimittis, and it goes like this:

> Master, now you are dismissing
>   Your servant in peace
> according to Your Word;
> for my eyes have seen Your
>   salvation,
> which You have prepared in the
> presence of all peoples,
> a light for revelation to the Gentiles
>   and for the glory of Your people
>   Israel. (vv. 29-31)

When Simeon finished his song he followed with a blessing (v. 34). This well-known leader, a pillar in the big city, gave a special blessing to this child of peasants and his young mother! Incredible. This was no religious fanatic. This was being done by one of Jerusalem's elite.

And then that paragon of spirituality, Anna, followed. The minute she saw Jesus this holy woman began to praise God for him and tell everybody about him and what he would do (v.38). Yes, both of these community pillars saw the Messiah, saw God himself, in that ordinary-looking child Jesus. No one in the temple, least of all Joseph and Mary either, could believe it (v. 33). It was an amazing series of events.

It certainly was amazing. That such things could happen, that such prominent religious people said and did these things in public, was indeed amazing. It was, after all, nothing but a poor insignificant baby with poor, humble parents who was the object of these community pillar's raves and praise. How could this infant possibly be regarded as if he were the Messiah, the Savior of Jews and Gentiles?

Oh, of course it's not so amazing to us. We know who this child is. We know he's the Son of God. But Simeon and Anna could not have known the course of his life like we do. They didn't **know** in advance what became of Jesus like we do. They didn't know the stories of Jesus' miracles, of his powerful preaching, or of his death and glorious resurrection. No, Simeon and Anna didn't **know** this about Jesus. But they did **believe** it. They didn't look at Jesus in terms of the way he appeared that day in the temple — an ordinary-looking baby of peasant parents. No, they looked at Jesus in terms of what he'd become — in terms of his future.

No, Simeon and Anna looked at the baby Jesus that day through the eyes of faith. That's the way faith works. Simeon and Anna show us that with faith, the beginning is nothing; the end is what counts. Remember that in your next new undertaking, Christian friends. The beginning is nothing; it's the end that counts. Martin Luther put it this way once in a sermon on this very biblical text:

> It [the story of Simeon and Anna] serves as an example of our faith; we, too, should learn how marvelous God's works are concerning us and that the beginning and end are quite dissimilar. The beginning is nothing; the end is everything. Just as the infant Christ does not appear very significant and yet, in the end, he became the Savior and light of all people. If Joseph and Mary had judged in accordance with what they saw they would not have regarded Christ as more than a poor little child. But they disregarded the external evidence... In like manner we, too, must disregard the external evidence when contemplating God's works and cling only to *his* words lest our eyes or senses offend us.[1]

The infant Jesus did not appear very significant. And yet in the end he became the Savior of the world! If Simeon and Anna had acted on the basis of present appearances they certainly would not have acted as they did with the baby Jesus — praising and worshiping him. No, the beginning is nothing for faith. Simeon and Anna acted on the basis of how Jesus would turn out in the end — when he'd reveal himself as God and set us human free from sin by rising from the dead on Easter and in all his glory at the Second Coming. For faith, it's the end that counts. The beginning (present appearances) is nothing; it's the end (how things come out in the future) that counts.

Why is it that way? Why is faith so future oriented and not so hung up on present appearances? Well Martin Luther's sermon on this text I already noted once said that faith is not concerned with present appearances. If you base faith on appearances, you are on your way to works righteousness, thinking that God only values what looks good. No, Christ and present appearances are at odds. That's why Christ saves sinners like you and me![2] He's making clear that salvation is not based on appearances, but on what Jesus does for us on Easter and at the end of time.

Think of it. Jesus himself took up a cross. Hardly what you would think a king and Lord would do. And then he proceeds to give you and me crosses too. He dispatches us into lives of sacrifice, to sacrifice some of the titillating things in the present for the sake of a future kingdom. He teaches us that most things people like us are so concerned about are nothing but foolishness and sin. That's why the beginning (present appearances) is nothing. That's why the end (what God does with our mess-ups and his rescue operations) is what counts.

Oh, but people like you and me too often don't live with this kind of future-oriented faith. We're not always disposed willingly to give up everything and suffer in the present for the sake of God's kingdom to be realized fully in the future. No, we're more likely to take offense at it all.

Sure, we are willing to praise God and worship him as long as he does what we want, and allows us to have what we want. Yes, but as soon as he demands something of us or makes things a little tough in the present, then we're likely to have had enough of this God. We are too prone to forget that the beginning (present appearances) is nothing, that it's the end (what God has in mind for us) that counts.

I know that some of you (myself included) are going to say that if **you** could have seen the infant Jesus and his mother in the flesh, like Simeon and Anna did, why *then* you would be willing to bless Christ joyfully with them. But that's all lies. No, Jesus' infancy and poverty, his humble appearance and background would have caused you and me to turn away had we lived back then. You and I too often prove this when we disregard the poverty and humble appearance of people who daily confront us, when we judge a book by its cover or people by their ethnicity instead of regarding it and the people we meet in light of the great plans God has for them in his kingdom.

Yes, just like we now flee from the cross, just like we avoid the humble and poor or complain about our present suffering, we would have reacted to Jesus in the same way had we met him in the temple that day along with Simeon and Anna. Why don't we honor and care about the poor? Why don't we accept our present sufferings? I'll tell you why. It's because we don't have Simeon's and Anna's faith. We make present appearances count for too much. When in God's plan of things, the beginning (present appearances) is nothing. It's the end that counts.

You know, our sinful preoccupation with present appearances even surfaces in our attitude towards good works and their necessity. Some of us still feel that you have to live a good life in order to be saved, in order to merit God's love. That's because we are too hung up on present appearances, too hung up on the beginning and not on the glorious end that God has in mind for us.

Somehow we have gotten this idea that God expects us to be righteous in the present, that we need to act righteously in the present or He will not save us. Oh, but you see, though God does not count us as sinners now in the present (Romans 3:21,25-26; 9:30; Galatians 3:6; Philippians 1:11), even though he counts us as righteous, he does not expect us to start manifesting this righteousness in the present. No, the full realization of righteousness is something that we will manifest in the future. It's in the future that you and I will be the perfect us. That point is explicitly made by Saint Paul in 2 Corinthians 9:10. It's in the same light that you have to read a message like Colossians 3:12-17. When the Bible especially the New Testament, gives directives about how Christians should live, it's really offering a description of how Christians will appear in the future.

This certainly fits with the Christian faith's future orientation. Our faith is future-oriented. It was the heart of Jesus' message. For faith, the beginning (the present) is nothing; it's the end that counts.

Keep this in mind. Keep the future-oriented faith of Simeon and Anna in today's gospel lesson. Keep it in mind the next time you encounter suffering, run across somebody who seems undesirable, or even the next time you're tempted to think you've done a good deed, that you've done enough for God or for your fellow human being. Keep it in mind that the beginning is nothing, for the end is what counts. Because what you're facing now does not ultimately matter. God's got other plans. Regard your neighbors, not as they appear now, but in light of what God is going to make of them in eternity. The suffering will not last forever. God has got other plans for you. And finally, don't forget you can never, on your own, do enough for God or someone else. Because in God's view, the beginning is nothing. It's the end that counts.

Oh what a good God we have. A God who sets us free from anxieties about the present, from our false perceptions about the present which often screw up our lives. We have a God who wipes those mistakes away. It's like Simeon and Anna told us: The beginning is nothing; it's the end (it's God's future) that counts. Praise God for the good and glorious future he has in mind for you. What a good and joyful security we have as we face the coming months.

NOTES
1. Martin Luther, "The Gospel for the Sunday After Christmas, Luke 2[:33-40]," in *Luther's Works*, Vol.52, ed. Hans Hillerbrand (Philadelphia: Fortress Press, 1974), p.104.
2. See *Ibid.*, pp.104,113.

Epiphany of the Lord
Matthew 2:1-12

The Light That Leads Us Away From Ourselves

Merry Christmas! Today (January 6) is Christmas for many Christians of Eastern Europe, Asia, and East Africa. In fact, January 6 was the first date for Christmas, and we only changed it centuries later to December 25. But even we Christians who celebrate on December 25 extend the celebration of Christmas right up to today, a festival we call Epiphany. Recall, we celebrated Christmas last Sunday here in church, even though it was December 31. That's why today's celebration of Epiphany, and the Bible story of The Wise Men traveling to find Jesus, relates to Christmas in the minds of many. No two ways about it: Christmas and Epiphany belong together.

You know the story as Matthew tells it: When Jesus was born in Bethlehem of Judea in the days when Herod was king (but the Romans ruled Israel), three Wise Men from the East came to Jerusalem looking for the king of the Jews. They had been following a star in the East. (We do know that there were Jewish settlements east of Israel in the first century in Parthia [part of Iran today].) They were probably not Jews, but could have been exposed to Jewish teachings about the Messiah.

Of course in coming to Jerusalem they went searching for the Messiah in the wrong place. But it was logical since Jerusalem was the capital, and you would expect a king to be born there. That's why they wound up consulting with Herod, figuring as king of Israel he would know (v.2). Well with the help of the chief priests and scribes (combining Micah 5:2 and 2 Samuel 5:2), Herod told them the Messiah would likely be born in Bethlehem (v.6).

Now there is more to the story of course, but first let's get clear on who the wise men were. Legend has it that they were kings. But historians have tended to conclude that they were probably astrologers — students of the stars. At the beginning of the New Testament era, astrologers were highly esteemed. They usually belonged to the upper class.[1]

We've already noted that these astrologers likely came from Parthia, ancestors of the Iranians. But there is a tradition in Christianity that at least one of them came from Africa and was Black. In fact, Martin Luther and his heritage have contended that this gentleman was Ethiopian![2] So we have in this Bible story a witness to the Black presence in the Bible!

The upper-class or upper middle-class status of astrologers in biblical times, coupled with some Old Testament passages that refer to kings who will worship the Messiah (Psalms 72:10, 15; Isaiah 49:7; 60:3,6,10) is what has led some people and even the hymn writer of "We Three Kings" to think (probably incorrectly) that the wise men were kings. No matter, these wise men (astrologers) came from good backgrounds. They had observed a radiance in the skies which modern astronomy believes could have been the result of conjunction from our earth-bound perspective of the planets Jupiter and Saturn, which last transpired in 7 BC and 4 BC. Does that give us another cue about the actual birthday of Jesus?

Anyhow, the wise men had learned to associate the radiant appearance of this conjunction of objects in space (they were sure it was a star) with the coming of the Messiah. Probably learned this from the Jews living in their region. The idea is at least suggested in the Jewish Bible, in the Old Testament, in Numbers 24:17. Taken from an oracle about whether Israel might rule over areas around the Jordan River, the text reads:

> a star shall come out of Jacob.
> and a scepter shall rise out of
> Israel;

(There are some hints of a star leading to the Messiah in Isaiah 60:1-6.)

No matter how the wise men came to know of the connections between what they observed in the sky and finding the Messiah. The point is that they came. They took the trip. They had relied on themselves and their insights, but in the end they found that their insights were not quite right (since Jerusalem was the wrong place to look).

That's the way God operates. We have a God who uses ordinary means to do great things, shines a light that teaches us to distrust ourselves and many of our instincts and expectations. This is what Christmas and the Incarnation teach us. The father of Existentialism, a nineteenth-century Danish Lutheran Søren Kierkegaard put it this way:

> In order that the union may be brought about, the God must therefore become the equal of such a one, and so *he* will appear in the likeness of the humblest. But the humblest is one who must serve others. And the God will appear in the form of a servant... Behold where *he* stands — the God! Where? There; so you cannot see *him*? He is the God; and yet *he* has not a resting-place for *his* head and *he* does not lean on any man lest *he* cause him to be offended... He is that God; and yet *his* eye rests upon humankind with deep concern...[3]

Think about these remarks. At Christmas, God took a lowly human being, not a wealthy ruler and became Incarnate in the lowly Jesus. His mother Mary certainly was not royalty. And then instead of getting born in the capital city, Jesus had his birth in a backwater town — in a **stable**. It's like Martin Luther once put it: "It is contradictory and shocking that a poor beggar, born in a lowly, poor place should be a ruler and Lord of the people of Israel."[4] See how God confounds the human ways and the human lights by operating in ways that nudge us away from ourselves and from human power? Let's get back to the Epiphany story, because this theme of confounding the world's and our own ways saturates the account.

Think of what happened when the wise men informed Herod of the child king who was to be born. Herod is reported to have feared this newborn child (v.3). A king fears a lowly, ordinary baby! The light of God leads us away from ourselves and our own power.

There is a sense in which Herod was a foreigner ruling Israel. He was certainly not considered a good Hebrew, for he was too Hellenized (influenced by Greek and Roman ways). Certainly when we consider Roman occupation in Jesus' day in Israel, the people were ruled by foreign elements. So it is with us today. Foreign elements rule our lives — foreign powers like greed, boredom, lust for power, and reputation, as well as a sense of being on a chaotic treadmill. Epiphany is a story of these powers shaking in their boots in face of the baby Jesus. The babe for whom the lights were sent by God, not the alien powers, is where the real meaning of life is to be found.

The starlight that the wise men followed, as interpreted by Herod's foreign courtiers, led them to that second-tier town Bethlehem, and we've already noted that the reason they would not expect that sort of setting for the birth of a king. They expected the messianic king to be born in the center of power. The centers of power in America are not typically the bearers of God's word. More than likely, God's ways are to be found among the poor and outcast, among ordinary people like us.

God's light led the wise men to the baby Jesus. The wealthy and educated paid him no homage. This is the heart of the Christmas message. But most of the time such humility is not our style. Commenting on this text, John Calvin noted how our stubborn self-centeredness is not inclined to such humility. He wrote:

> In a word, so long as wicked men think that it is taking nothing from themselves, they will yield to God and to *scripture* some degree of relevance. But when Christ comes into conflict with ambition, covetousness, pride, misplaced confidence, hypocrisy, and deceit they immediately forget all modesty, and break out into rage.[5]

We are too often mired in self-righteousness as we gleefully compare our morality, spiritual, psychological health to our neighbors. As Martin Luther once put it: We "stink of pure self-esteem and self-conceit."[6] We are so hung up on ourselves that a day's attention to the Christ-child (if that long) is about all we can stand. We need the light of God, like the one he used to guide the wise men, to lead us away from ourselves.

Thank God, sin and self-preoccupation do not have the final word. That's why we want to celebrate Epiphany. The wise men were not perfect. Yet God summoned them to Bethlehem by the star, just as he summons you and me into the ordinary "Bethlehems" of life. The miracle of the Epiphany and of Christmas is that the light of Christ shines even for and on all too ordinary sinners like us! Epiphany sends a message like the Christmas word. Confronted as we are by the lights of Christ, by the compelling love of God in the ordinary, lowly things of life, you and I will be led away from ourselves as well and all our selfish hang-ups fall down and collapse into the arms of our loving God.

The light of God in Christ Jesus blinds you and me to everything in life and its temptations. May that light blind you lots in the year ahead.

NOTES
1. For this assessment, see Eduard Schweizer, *The Good News According To Matthew*, trans. David E. Green (Atlanta: John Knox Press, 1066), p.38.
2. Martin Luther, *Lectures on the Psalms* (1513-1515), in *Luther's Works*, Vol.10, ed. Hilton Oswald (Saint Louis: Concordia, 1974),pp. 412-413.
3. Søren Kierkegaard, *Philosophical Fragments*, trans. David Swenson (Princeton, NJ: Princeton University Press, 1967), pp. 39-40.
4. Martin Luther, "Epiphany — First Sermon," (1532), *The Complete Sermons of Martin Luther*, Vol.5, ed. John N. Lenker (Grand Rapids, MI: Baker, 2000), p. 205.
5. John Calvin, *Commentary On a Harmony of the Evangelists, Matthew, Mark, and Luke* (1553), in *Calvin's Commentaries*, Vol.XVI/1, trans. William Pringle (Grand Rapids, MI: Baker, 2005), p. 333.
6. Martin Luther, "The Gospel for the Festival of the Epiphany" (1522), in *Luther's Works*, Vol.52, ed. Hans Hillerbrand (Philadelphia: Fortress Press, 1974), p. 199.

A Fresh Start Jesus' Way

Imagine the gossip in first-century Israel about that prophet named John the Baptist. The man seemed crazy. He'd been traveling all over the countryside, especially in the wilderness, like a nomad. Had a strange diet — just eating locusts and wild honey. He also wore camel's hair with a leather belt (vv. 4,6).[1] This baptismal ritual of his and talk of repentance sound like those crazy sectarians around the Dead Sea. And we know how crazy they are, leaving civilization to go out and live like nomads.[2]

It's interesting that baptism was controversial among contemporaries of Jesus. Hebrews did not practice it, except for the community that produced the Dead Sea Scrolls known as Essenes. It's not that way for us today, is it? There is nothing controversial about baptism. We pretty much take it for granted. If only we could return to that way of looking at things, we and the church would be a lot better off.

Many of us know the hard times the church is facing in America. Church membership in all the mainline denominations is in decline, and the Black church as well as most evangelical denominations are barely breaking even. We have not really achieved our equilibrium in our own personal lives since the pandemic. A 2021 Gallup poll found that just 38% of Americans feel good about life. Things have not improved in the past two years, as we have been progressively going down on that statistic since before the pandemic. In a late 2021 poll conducted by Zippa Research just after the "Great Resignation" (of millions of workers) that we heard so much about, it was found that only 49% of us are very satisfied with our jobs.[3]

Let me tell you about John and Ruth who belong to a congregation across town a lot like ours. This middle-aged couple, situated financially kind of like most members of our congregation, has a lot to worry about. Sure, they had raises, but inflation is playing heck with their budget and the jobs aren't all that satisfying. As the years rolled by John was wondering if what he was doing really mattered or would really leave a legacy. Speaking of legacy, college-costs are also rising astronomically, and they did not want to saddle their kids with too much college debt. On top of that, both their parents were aging, and Ruth's widowed mother was increasingly less able to care for herself.

Added to all this is a feeling that the relationship was not working well. Both wished it could be better, but both felt trapped by old habits. John and Ruth didn't feel like they had realized or even sought their dreams (though their lifestyle was certainly a lot more orthodox with a higher standard of living than John the Baptist and that native of Nazareth John baptized).

When dreams don't feel fulfilled or when you are just running to keep up the pace and lost a sense of your dreams like what happened to John and Ruth (and to so many Americans), life feels empty. Joy and fulfillment are missing. Dreams, openness to the future, make life meaningful. In one of his speeches, Patrick Henry was thought to have said, "I like the dreams of the future better than the history of the past." And to well-known nineteenth-century American Episcopalian Bishop Phillips Brooks (who wrote the lyrics to "O Little Town of Bethlehem") are attributed similar sentiments in the quote: "Very strange is the quality of our human nature which decrees that unless we feel a future before us we do not live completely in the present."

The problem with life (call it original sin) is that you and I get so caught up in the present challenges of just maintaining ourselves, get trapped by our past ways of operating, that we close the door to the future. And there seems to be no escape. The past and the present become like a vice, squeezing the life-blood and spirit out of us, until other options, other ways of existing outside the mode of life we're in now, just don't exist. Our personal lives reflect these dynamics. But institutions, including churches, get sucked into that kind of behavior. No accident that businesses which are not flexible don't survive. And it says a lot about the church in America that, despite the marked growth of the religiously unaffiliated (the so-called "nones") only a handful of denominations have created programs to address these dynamics.[4]

Well Jesus and John the Baptist broke out of the boxes in which their present circumstances tried to put them. They found a way to make fresh starts. Remember how outrageous John the Baptist's behavior seemed to be. And of course as one of John's followers and later in the way he lived, Jesus went against the grain, provided a fresh-start alternative to the social expectations placed on Hebrew men in his day.

What's intriguing here is that a big part of John's new start alternative is baptism! Baptism is how Jesus started his ministry. Hear that? Want a fresh start? Want some alternatives to a life that's not been fulfilling? John the Baptist and Jesus point you and me to baptism.

"Baptism? Oh come on, preacher. How can getting bathed in a little bit of water along with some words make a difference like you've been describing?" Well, remember that compared to historic Judaism which did not baptize adherents, baptism was something new in its origins. And note that it's how Jesus started his ministry. It sure did make a difference in the way he lived his life for his final three years after his first thirty.

Famed New Testament scholar Rudolf Bultmann put it well when he noted that baptism in the first century was a liturgical action or rite which pointed to the end time, to the kingdom of God.[5] To be baptized is to be living in the reality of the coming kingdom, to live in a future-oriented way, no longer bound by the past or by present experience. The New Testament itself makes this point too. In Romans 6 (v. 5) Paul speaks of baptism in terms of being born again, regeneration. Even churches which don't believe you are born again in baptism (like Catholics, Eastern Christians, Lutherans, and some Episcopalians), but believe baptism is just a symbol or seal still link the sacrament to this idea of being born again, that you are made new and given a fresh start. Martin Luther once put it this way: Baptism, he said:

> ... not only announces this new life but also produces, begins, and exercises it. In baptism we are given the grace, Spirit, and strength to suppress the old creature so that the new may come forth and grow strong.[6]

In his *Small Catechism* he even said that in baptism "daily a new person is to come forth and rise up.."[7] In other words, baptism has an impact on who you are. You are reborn in baptism with certain gifts which make you disposed to breaking with the past and seeking fresh starts. It is just like when you're born, the genes you have been given dispose you to certain behaviors. Some of us are born with musical or athletic talents. In the baptism Jesus gives you and me, we are now disposed to living Christ's way, to venture into fresh starts and new beginnings, boldly willing to challenge the anxieties that can arise when you challenge the status quo and refuse to live any longer with the discontent of the present.

What does this new life, this fresh start given us in baptism look like? Again that great New Testament scholar Rudolf Bultmann provides useful insight on what this fresh start we get from Jesus in the waters of baptism looks like. He writes that it is ... to be open to God's future which is really imminent for every one of us; to be prepared for this future which can come as a thief in the night when we do not expect it...[8] Then he added about this fresh start that Christ provided:

> Therefore free openness to the future is freedom to take anxiety upon ourselves... If it is true that the Christian faith involves free openness to the future, then it is freedom from anxiety in face of nothing...[9]

Like I said already, it takes courage to break with the past or with your situation in the present. This is the anxiety Bultmann said must be overcome if we are going to make fresh starts and be open to the future. And this is what Jesus, what his baptism provided — the courage, the freedom, to live boldly! In baptism we get changed. It's like we noted already how Martin Luther said: baptism gives you and me the "strength to suppress the old creature so that the new may come forth and grow strong."[10]

Hall of Fame Baseball Pitcher Bob Feller once offered a description of baseball which is readily applicable to the future orientation Christians have been given by Jesus in our baptisms. According to Feller:

> Every day is a new opportunity. You can build on yesterday's success or leave failure behind and start over. That's the way life is, with a new game every day...

This sort of looking forward-way of life has other benefits, and remember living with Jesus' baptism launches you into a life like this. Neurobiological research has shown that an openness to new ideas and activities can stimulate the brain to make new neural connections which lead to release of neurochemicals which both leads us to experience happiness and impede the aging process.[11] These biological dynamics may explain why Americans trapped in the status quo are so unhappy, according to the polls. But these data certainly provide a wonderful testimony to our faith. Live out your baptism, live the life of fresh starts that Jesus provides, the way John the Baptist lived, and life will be a lot better and happier.

Feeling trapped and burned out? Christians, those feelings are lies! Your baptism, Jesus' fresh start, has made you and me new, forward-looking, daring people. The next time you feel trapped or burned out, remember you're baptized and brand new, somebody inclined to seek fresh starts. Hold on to that insight as you go through 2024! It really is a brand new year.

NOTES

1. For the prophetic significance of these activities and attire, see the first two paragraphs of the Advent 2 sermon.
2. See *Ibid.*, esp. n.1.
3. The Gallup poll result is reported in Harry Enten, "American happiness hits record lows," *CNN Politics* (feb.2, 2022), at cnn.com/2022.92.02.politics/unhappiness-americans'gallup-analysis/index.html. Also see Jack Flynn, "43 Incredible Job Satisfaction Statistics [2022]: Average Job Satisfaction in the US" (Dec. 1, 2021).
4. See my *Ever Hear of Feuerbach? That's Why American and European Christianity Are in Such a Funk!* (Eugene, OR: Cascade, 2020), pp.23-24.
5. Rudolf Bultmann, *Theology of the New Testament*, Vol.1, Kendrick Grobel (New York: Charles Scribner's Sons, 1951), pp.39-40.
6. Martin Luther, *The Large Catechism* (1529), *The Book of Concord*, eds. Robert Kolb and Timothy J. Wengert (Minneapolis: Fortress Press, 2000), p.466.
7. Martin Luther, *The Small Catechism* (1529), *The Book of Concord*, p.360.
8. Rudolf Bultmann, *Jesus Christ and Mythology* (New York: Charles Scribner's Sons, 1958), p.31.
9. *Ibid.*, pp.77-78.
10. See n.6.
11. Sherwin Nuland, *The Art of Aging: A Doctor's Prescription for Well-Being* (New York: Random House, 2007), pp.34ff.

Epiphany 2
John 1:43-51

Do You Need A Miracle To Follow Jesus?

Jesus and his first group of converts were on a journey to Galilee (v. 43). On the way they encountered a man Philip, who was from the same town as Jesus' first recruits, Andrew and Peter (v. 44). Philip came upon a man named Nathaniel and began to confess the faith to him. Philip told Nathaniel that he and his cohorts had found the one whom Moses in the law and all the prophets had written about, and this man he added was Jesus of Nazareth (v.45). Of course Nathaniel, reflecting the attitudes of his day, responded by asking whether anything good could come out of Nazareth like Jesus did (v.46a). But in any case, Philip urged Nathaniel again to meet Jesus (v.46b).

Then Jesus greeted Nathaniel as if he knew him, claiming that Nathaniel was an Israelite in whom there was no deceit (v.47, probably a reference to the fact that the man named Israel [Jacob] received his original blessing through deceit [Genesis 27:35]). This shocked Nathaniel who challenged Jesus regarding how Jesus could have known him. Jesus explained that he had seen Nathaniel before Philip had, and the result was that Nathaniel, now convinced of Jesus' supernatural powers, confessed him to be Son of God and king of Israel (vv.48-49).

Jesus then challenged Nathaniel, asking him whether he now believed because of what Jesus had told him about who he was. *Great things are to be seen*, Jesus added. For Nathaniel and others would see the heavens opened, with the angels of God ascending and descending on Jesus the Son of Man (vv.50-51). (In this version of the gospel, Jesus seemed to be portrayed as the link between heaven and earth [3:13; 5:26-27].) Miracles aren't such a big deal, our gospel lesson seems to say, and besides, we haven't seen anything yet.

Do you agree with John's version of Jesus, agree that miracles are not a good reason for believing? In the most recent poll on the subject back in 2008, nearly 80% of Americans claimed they still believe in miracles. Now we have to assume that that number is lower with the deaths of the greatest generation and baby boomers in the last fifteen years, but even if the percentage is still above 50%, the number believing in miracles does not seem to have much impact on faith, given the decline of American Christianity and the growth of the religiously unaffiliated since the 1960s.

Let me raise the issue with you this way: Would having some miracle performed in front of you make it easier for you to believe? If you're honest, of course, miracles are something that would help. But our problem is that we are so blind that we miss the miracles that happen daily before our very eyes.

There are a number of miracles in our gospel story for today, but the problem is that only faith can see them (kind of like without penetrating faith you miss a lot of miracles in life). The first miracle is that Jesus' disciples were not drawn from the upper class. He calls everyone and anyone — even the members of this congregation hearing this sermon. Saint Augustine made that point, around 1,200 years ago. He wrote:

> No noble was chosen in the first place, no learned man, because God chose the weak things of the world that *he* might confound the strong.[1]

God gets the job done with unworthy, ordinary people like you and me. It's time we began to realize this.

Sometimes church work and community service don't seem like that big of a deal. But in this light we can see that they really are greater miracles than any healing or prosperity God might confer on us. No, what's really miraculous is that God would actually use us through our deeds to carry on his sacred work!

As for the second miracle, the quick response of Nathaniel and the other first disciples is miraculous. No real reason was given for following Jesus. Think about what makes you a Christian. Reason just gives way sometimes to the decision or to the fact that you always were Christian, just raised that way. How interesting/odd that the most important thing you have decided in life (having to do with your eternal salvation) happened for many of us through ordinary-seeming events in life. That the divine Holy Spirit has been working through such ordinary means is miraculous.

Who needs miracles? Miracles are all around us. Martin Luther made that clear in a sermon he preached on the gospel of Mark. He claimed:

> We are so accustomed to find that grain grows out of the earth annually, and we are so blinded by this that we pay no attention to it; for what we daily see and hear we do not consider a miracle. And yet it is as great a miracle... as Christ's feeding the multitude with seven loaves.[2]

Okay, if we don't need miracles because they are all around us, why were there miracles performed in biblical times? Again Martin Luther gave us insight:

> God will perform no miracles so long as problems can be solved by means of other gifts *he* has bestowed on us.[3]

More modern people, with more sophisticated means do not need visible, supernatural miracles as much as followers of Jesus in the biblical era did. Saint Augustine also offered another sound reason why the supernatural miracles of biblical times are not continuing. He wrote:

> We have heard that our predecessors, at a stage in faith on the way from temporal to eternal things, followed visible miracles... When the Catholic Church had been founded and diffused throughout the whole world, on the one hand miracles were not allowed to continue till our time, lest the mind should always seek visible things, and the human race should grow cold by becoming accustomed to the things which when they were novelties kindled its faith.[4]

Isn't it neat that the struggles some of us in the twenty-first century have with wondering why the Bible miracles are not still happening is a question Christians have struggled with since the dawn of Protestantism and since the fifth century? And these great thinkers of the faith are telling us to chill out on this matter. There are good reasons the miracles today are not like in Bible times.

Of course, we've already seen how miracles are still happening. And it seems that you don't even have to be a Christian to see miracles in everyday life. The founder of Buddhism, Gautama Siddhartha, said it well: "If we could see the miracle of a single flower clearly, our whole life would change."[5] And it is believed that Albert Einstein said much the same thing, contending that "There are only two ways to live your life. One is as though nothing is a miracle. The other is as though everything is a miracle." Buddha is right. Life is so different, so beautiful, when seen as a miracle. For then you appreciate and cherish the things of life so much more when you see life that way.

Speaking of miracles, how about those times when life feels like it is closing in on you? Think of the financial pressures of our time, the personal losses, wars, the feeling that none of us is likely to be alive 100 years from now. We have all had those feelings and experiences, yet somehow have gotten the courage to get up the next morning, to keep on going. Weren't those moments of perseverance and strength to continue sheer gifts of God, miracles?

Martin Luther claimed that our Bible text for today has some special advice for coping with moments of despair. In a sermon he claimed:

> In such circumstances our dear Lord wants us to raise our eyes upward and to remember, when we find this world too cramped for us, that here we are only guests, as it were, in an inn, that we hold citizenship elsewhere, namely, in heaven. In view of this we can resign ourselves to our lot.[6]

The things of this earth are just an inn, like the rooms we rent when travelling, and so don't matter that much if we lose them. Our home lies up ahead in heaven.

Speaking of heaven, keep in mind Jesus' claim that the heavens would be opened (v.51). Luther also has a helpful insight about what Jesus meant. He explained it this way:

> ...we are already in heaven, where someday our eternal praise of God and our hallelujahs will resound. Even now we make a beginning by singing to God constant songs of praise and hallelujahs that indicate what we shall be doing.[7]

When we praise God, as is happening in this very worship service, it truly is a great miracle. It is doing on earth what happens in heaven; in worship and service to God a little bit of heaven is right here on earth.

Who needs miracles? Who needs miracles to confirm faith? The next time you feel tempted to despair about if all this Christian stuff is true or envy the disciples for actually seeing miracles (wish you had been in first-century Israel to see them too), keep in mind how many miracles you can see every day, how the very thing we do every Sunday is to get a glimpse of miracles right here on earth! There'll be a lot of miracles coming your way this week. Don't miss them.

NOTES

1. Augustine, *Homilies On the Gospel of John* (416), *Nicene and Post-Nicene Fathers*, First Series, Vol.7, ed. Philip Schaff (2nd print.; Peabody, MA: Hendrickson, , 1995), p.54.
2. Martin Luther, "Sermon on Mark 8:1-9," *What Luther Says*, ed. Edward Plass (Saint Louis: Concordia, 1959), p.954
3. Martin Luther, *To the Councilmen of All the cities of Germany That They Establish and Maintain Christian Schools* (1524), *What Luther Says*, p.955.
4. Augustine, *Of True Religion* (390), in *Augustine: Earlier Writings*, ed. John H. S. Burleigh (Philadelphia: Westminst3er, 1953), p.248.
5. See Jack Kornfield, ed., *Buddha's Little Instruction Book* (New York: Random House, 1994).
6. Martin Luther, *Several Chapters of St. John the Evangelist* (1537), in *Luther's Works*, Vol.22, trans. Martin Bertram (Saint Louis: Concordia, 1957), p.205.
7. *Ibid.*, p.211.

It's Urgent: The Kingdom Of God Is At Hand!

You know the old adage: Don't put off until tomorrow what you can do today. Well, it was just after the arrest of John the Baptist. Jesus was beginning his activity in Galilee (v.14). He started off with the exciting word that "The time is fulfilled and the kingdom of God has come near; repent and believe in the good news! (v.15) The kingdom of God has come near, Jesus proclaimed. Don't wait until tomorrow. It's urgent. Don't put off until tomorrow what you can do today.

Jesus was passing along that large lake called the Sea of Galilee. He saw Simon and Simon's brother Andrew fishing. And Jesus said they should follow him, and he would make them fishers of men (v16). Simon and Andrew stopped fishing and began to follow Jesus (v.17). Don't put off until tomorrow what you can do today. Immediately after this Jesus saw James the son of Zebedee and his brother John, fishermen who were in their boat mending their nets (v.19).

Again Jesus called them right away. Immediately they too left their boats, left behind their father and his hired hands, and followed Jesus (v.20). No putting off until tomorrow what they could do that day. When you follow Jesus, things are urgent.

There's another story, about Harvey and Mary locked in an unhappy marriage. Their kids were falling in with the wrong crowd and neither partner was doing the jobs he or she had dreamed of in their youth. Still in their late thirties when these realities became apparent, they took no action, feeling they both had enough on their plates and just felt too paralyzed to act. The years rolled by. Things got worse. The marriage was gone, two of the three kids in trouble, all the extra expenses of the divorce and two households, plus a lot of unhappy lives. Don't put it off until tomorrow. It's urgent! The kingdom of God has come near!

It's obvious, isn't it? Jesus' way is to be urgent. Putting things off is not God's way. Martin Luther King Jr. was right when he once said, "We are confronted today with the fierce urgency of the now."[1] American self-help author H. Jackson Brown Jr. had it right: "You must take action now that will move you toward your goals. Develop a sense of urgency in your life."

Without urgency, life gets routine and boring. You just stay stuck in circumstances that probably don't satisfy. The longer you stay there, the harder it gets to move on. But when you heed the call of Jesus, move with him into the future, life looks a lot better. Don't put it off until tomorrow. It's urgent! The kingdom of God has come near!

Consider the disciples in today's gospel story. John Calvin once did a wonderful job of describing who they were:

> Christ selected rough mechanics, persons not only destitute of learning, but inferior in capacity that *he* might train, or renew them by the power of *his* Spirit, so as to excel all the wise men of the world. He intended to humble, in this manner, the pride of the flesh... to humble the pride of those who think that heaven is not open to the unlearned.[2]

Yes, Simon Peter, Andrew, James, and John were just ordinary men. But they responded to Jesus' call **immediately**, with alacrity and look what became of them. These so-ordinary Hebrew peasants have become world famous for nearly 2000 years! By God's grace that moved them to respond they knew that, "Now is the time. Don't put it off until tomorrow." The kingdom of God had come near to them.

Sometimes we make excuses for not doing the right thing, claiming we are not ready yet or not sure of our motives. Well, God will use you to do good for somebody even the next time you don't have it in your heart to do so. Again John Calvin was on target when he claimed that God can use us even prior to our repentance.[3]

World-famous artist and inventor Leonardo da Vinci had it right, as it is reported he once reportedly claimed that, "I have been impressed with the urgency of doing. Knowing is not enough; we must apply. Being willing is not enough; we must do." It doesn't matter if you are willing to do it, have the right motives. When it comes to the work of God, "Just do it" (by God's grace)! It's urgent. The kingdom of God has come near. I love the way the Methodist founder John Wesley once put it" "Happy are they who follow Christ at the first call."[4]

Christians have this future orientation. A statement attributed to evangelical pastor and sociology professor Tony Campolo was on target: "Your past is important, but it is not nearly as important to your present as the way you see your future."

Our nation, indeed Western society, needs this future-oriented perspective. Books are being written questioning whether democracy has a future.[5] A poll conducted as recently as late 2021 by National Public Radio found that 64% of Americans felt that the United States' democracy is in crisis. Meanwhile the middle-class keeps getting squeezed, while poverty, racism, and gun violence continue. Oh, but most times all we do is convene committees to discuss these matters, or let the market play out (no matter how many lives are lost to the violence or to poverty and hunger while we wait).

What Martin Luther King Jr. said nearly seven decades ago is still correct today. It's what Jesus' actions and the response of the disciples were teaching us. In his famed 1963 speech in Washington, King spoke of the "fierce urgency of now." Knowing America had the resources (we still have the resources to address our problems today), he reminded us that the dream (the vision of the kingdom of God) promised equality and resources for all.[6] Five years later in his final Sunday sermon delivered, he included ending war and overcoming poverty in that dream (calling it a revolution).[7] We've still got wars and poverty, and all the other problems Dr. King addressed. Can we afford, can our nation afford, to wait another six or seven decades to change all this? Jesus and his disciples don't advocate waiting. They saw the vision; they knew what God wanted — and they did it!

Back to Harvey and Mary, who had put off the tough decisions about their relationship, their kids, and their lives. Isn't there someone in this congregation who has been at a crossroads like them, and postponed the decision? Maybe you are even encountering situations like that right now. But even if your personal life is not at a crossroads, surely the challenges our nation and our community face are urgent.

Our gospel story makes clear that we dare not wait, or the tragic destinies of Harvey and Mary (divorce, children gone wrong, decreased resources) could be how we and our nation end up. At the very least, just living well enough alone results in a life of boredom or progressive discontent, and finally the grave accompanied with it has a lot of regrets. Jesus and his disciples give us a better option. With God's grace, respond! Jump on the opportunity!

Our nation cannot continue indefinitely with all the poverty, ethnic, and international tensions. Let's work for change: It's urgent! The kingdom of God is at hand.

There is good news that is inextricably linked to this challenge to act urgently. We do not have to worry about whether we have the strength alone to take urgent risks of faith. John Calvin and others have taught us that the repentance involved in responding to Jesus' call to urgent decision is rooted in God's action and the work of the Holy Spirit. As the reformer put it:

> The Lord commands you to turn to *himself*; but as you cannot accomplish this by your own *endeavors*, *he* promises the Spirit of regeneration, and therefore you must receive this grace...[8]

When it comes to urgent decision-making, chill out. God does the heavy lifting.

Yes, don't put it off until tomorrow. It's urgent. The kingdom of God is on horizon! And the Holy Spirit is right by your side to prod you and me to do the right thing.

NOTES
1. Martin Luther King Jr., "Beyond Vietnam," in *A Call to Conscience: The Landmark Speeches of Martin Luther King Jr.*, eds. Clayborne Carson and Kris Shepard (New York: Warner Books, 2009), p.162.
2. John Calvin, *Commentary On a Harmony of the Evangelists, Matthew, Mark, and Luke* (1553), in *Calvin's Commentaries*, Vol.XVI/1, trans. William Pringle (Grand Rapids, MI: Baker, 2005). p.243.
3. *Ibid.*, p.225.
4. John Wesley, *Commentary On the Bible*, ed. G. Roger Schoenhals (Grand Rapids, MI: Francis Asbury, 1990), p.425.
5. For example, see Steven Levitski and Daniel Ziblatt, *How Democracies Die: What History Reveals About Our Future* (New York: Broadway Books, 2019); Yaecha Mounk, *The People vs. Democracy: Why Out Freedom Is in Danger and How To Save It* (Cambridge, MA: Harvard University Press, 2019).
6. Martin Luther King Jr., "I Have a Dream," (1963).
7. Martin Luther King Jr., "Remaining Awake Through a Great Revolution" (March 31, 1968)
8. Calvin, p.225.

Living With The Authority Of Jesus

Authority! Authority is one of those funny words in the English language that doesn't get used that often. But at the same time it is a word that most of us understand. We talk about hoodlums and gangsters getting in trouble with the authorities; we say of politicians and rulers that they have great authority, and we sit up and listen when somebody speaks with authority. To have authority means that you can get done what needs to be done, because authority means clout. Our gospel lesson for today talks about Jesus' authority. Now that is a word that not many of us have ever thought much about in connection with Jesus. But Mark sure must have thought it was important. Because here in the very first chapter of his gospel he tells us a story that's clearly intended to show the great authority Jesus has. But what kind of authority is it? What does it mean to talk about Jesus' authority?

It was a hot, sticky summer day in Capernaum, on the coast of the Sea of Galilee (though rain was not as common in town as in most of Israel). Just the same it was Saturday, the sabbath, so you and your family had to get to the synagogue for the morning worship services. On the way you met some friends with big news. It seemed that Jonah Bar-Simon's wife Naomi had just given birth to twins and the whole town was up in arms about the blessed event. With news like that it's no wonder that you and your friends got to the synagogue a little late. Quietly the four of you snuck in the door and found a seat in the back. But something seemed strange. Up front, along with the rabbis, there was some strange guy, kind of on the short side with a beard. Funny, he was not dressed like any rabbi you've ever seen. Looked more like a working man instead, a carpenter or a tent-maker maybe. But man he sure seemed to know his Bible. Just listen to him spouting those passages. He must have been one of those "big-shot rabbis" from Jerusalem. But then what the heck was he doing in our little town? And on top of that there was something about the way he talked. You can't quite put your finger on it, but it's not like any other person you've ever heard. Maybe it was his confidence. It seemed like he was just sure what he was saying was absolutely right, and no questions asked (v.22).

Suddenly, though, your thoughts were shattered by loud screams coming from your left. Oh no, it was that same crazy old man you had seen before, screaming like a loon (v.23). That guy had no business walking around the streets loose. He got those screaming fits, and he did not know what he was saying. His family should have put him away years ago. And now here he was disturbing worship.

Well, you said to yourself, maybe the stranger could get that crazy old man to quiet down. The disrupter was screaming, "What have you to do with us, Jesus of Nazareth? Have you come to destroy us? I know who you are, the holy one of God." (v.24) Oh man, you think, this guy is really off his trolley. But wait, the stranger was saying something to him. Something was happening; something weird. There was another loud scream and then complete silence (vv. 25-26).

And now what was happening? The crazy old man was addressing this stranger he called Jesus of Nazareth and he was also talking with those around him. He looked all right; he seemed normal. It was hard to believe. That stranger did something to the old man. What did that fellow up there have going for him? Not only could he preach with authority, but it almost seemed like he was some kind of a healer to boot! Why it was just amazing...amazing.

It was a gray day in our town, pretty much like usual during winter months, and you've just had to get that present Uncle Harvey gave you exchanged. But what a hassle there would be in exchanging it! Those sales clerks had been giving you the run-around all morning since you got into the store. All you heard was, "That's not my job" "Wrong department." "Try upstairs." Finally, though, you managed to get into the office of one of the assistant store-managers, the one in charge of customer relations. He was a very pleasant young man, somebody who really seemed to care. On top of that he was a good listener, smiling agreeably while you told the whole story. Finally when you got done he shook his head sadly. "Golly," he said, "I'd really like to help you get this done." (And it really seemed like he would like to help.) "But I just don't have any power when it comes to exchanges like this; I just do not have the authority."

The first of our two little stories is a loose retelling of today's gospel lesson. The second is a story about something that has probably happened to almost all of us at one time or another. Because almost all of us have run into people who seemingly would have liked to have helped us, but couldn't because they just didn't have the clout. Now the question is: What do these stories have to do with each other? Quite a bit, I'd say. In fact these two stories have enough points of contact that people often get them quite confused, so we take the main character of the gospel lesson story, Jesus Christ, and confuse him with the nice polite assistant store-manager who didn't have any authority. Just like the people in today's Bible lesson who heard Jesus preach and saw him perform that healing, we're so amazed, so shocked, that even though we've seen the great things Jesus has done we just can't seem to believe that he could have that kind of authority.

Let's pause here for a moment, so you can be sure what I am saying. I do not think for a minute that anybody here this morning does not believe in Jesus Christ. I am sure that when we recite the creed in a few minutes, everybody will sincerely believe what they are saying. Yes, in our own way we all believe that Christ rose from the dead and that because of this we can now live new lives free from our old hang-ups. Yes, we all believe it, but we are not quite sure Jesus has the authority or the power to make a difference in our lives.

For instance, as human beings all of us wonder what's going to happen to us when we die. And because we may not be sure what's in store for us, death becomes something that many of us fear. All of us assembled today are Christians, right? And Christians believe that because of Jesus Christ's death and resurrection, death is not the end, but the beginning of eternal life. Despite the fact that we Christians should have an answer to the question of what is waiting for us after death, I can't tell you the number of times over the years I've overheard faithful Christians wonder out loud whether there was anything beyond the grave. That does not mean people like that are hypocrites, not sincerely committed to Christian faith. No, not at all. I think almost all Christians have moments when they are not really sure (myself included). And in those moments it is not so much that we have lost our faith in Christ. It's just that in those moments we are not quite sure about the authority of Jesus, his clout to pull off what he says he can, really deliver us from death. His intentions are good, but can he really do what he says?

The resurrection is not the only promise Jesus made that we Christians often can't quite believe. The message of Jesus Christ is a word not just of eternal life, but of love. Because God loves us, the little ups and downs of life should not impact us quite as much, for we know God cares for us. No, they should not affect us, but they do. Maybe it's the aggravation that comes with a household appliance or car on the blink. Life feels like a hassle, and we may wonder where God and his love are. He just doesn't seem to have the authority to help us.

Am I the only one in the building this morning who's gone through times like this? I doubt it. Maybe it was not car problems, a bad mark in school, fight with family members, layoffs at work, or just a general feeling of inferiority and self-hate. All of us sometimes feel life has let us down. Not that we stop believing in Jesus, but we have forgotten or stopped being confident that he has the authority to help us. We turn him into that helpless assistant manager of the store.

Here's what Martin Luther said:

> But now, since *he* [Christ] has given *himself* for you, what can terrify you?... Oh, here is great sure security... Christ will certainly not waver. He is firm enough.[1]

How can we doubt Jesus' authority when we have such security? Our gospel lesson reminds us of the authority he displayed here on earth even before he was glorified. Not sure about God's love and its clout? The great ancient African theologian Augustine sings the praises of the authority of God's love:

> Now "the love of God" is said to be shed abroad in our hearts, not because *he* loves us, but because He makes *us lovers* of *himself*.[2]

God's love is actually so authoritative that it changes us. God and Jesus clearly have the authority to love you and me and change us. Still have doubts about God loving you and the authority of God's love? Hear Martin Luther's words in a 1532 sermon:

> God *himself* is *love*, and *his* being is nothing but pure love. Therefore if anyone wanted to draw and picture God in a telling way, he would have to draw a picture that showed nothing but love, as though the divine nature were nothing but an intense fire and fervor of a love that has filled heaven and earth.[3]

Hear that? God's love is an intense fire filling heaven and earth. That's authority. God in Jesus Christ has authority to set the universe on fire with his love. Yes, Jesus has the authority to change your and my lives, to fill them with love. No doubts need remain. You and I and the universe are now and forevermore on fire with God's love. Like an unquenchable fire can't help but change things, so God's love in Jesus has this kind of authority in your life, in our community, to change things.

NOTES
1. Martin Luther, "Christmas Sermon" (1522), in *What Luther Says*, ed. Edward Plass (Saint Louis: Concordia, 1959), p.699.
2. Augustine, *On the Spirit and the Letter* (412), in *Nicene and Post-Nicene Fathers*, First Series, Vol.5, ed. Philip Schaff (2nd printing; Peabody, MA: Hendrickson, 1995), p.108.
3. Martin Luther, "Sermon on 1 John 4:16-21" (1532), in *What Luther Says*, p.819.

Presentation of the Lord
Luke 2:22-40

Present Appearances Don't Matter As Much As Christ's Light And The Dream

Late in December we considered like we are today the story of how as the firstborn son of his family, Jesus was to be presented at the temple in Jerusalem, to be consecrated, designated as holy to the Lord. Also in accord with Leviticus 12, Mary was presented for a purification, and a sacrifice of turtledoves and young pigeons was offered (since the family obviously could not afford a sheep to sacrifice) (vv. 22-24). Then we heard the story about how the aging and venerable community pillars Simeon and Anna were present, and were moved by the Holy Spirit to confess the baby Jesus as the long-awaited Messiah. When we studied this story last time it was part of a continuation of the Christmas story. Well it is still Christmas and the Incarnation which we celebrate with this story. But today's a different festival, the festival of The Presentation of our Lord, a celebration that dates back at least to the fourth century. Now our Catholic brothers and sisters tend to focus more on the part of the story about how in the temple Mary received rites of purification (v.22). This makes the Presentation a festival for celebrating Mary as well.

We'll stick to our festival's ancient roots today and just focus on Jesus. Focus on Jesus and how these venerable community members reacted. In its origin the festival was also a time of penance, of confessing how we've been blowing it and receiving forgiveness. Extra lights and candles were also added to the altar since everything was about Christ.[1]

Okay, what does it mean to say that we put more light on the subject? It means that things become clearer. That's what Jesus, that's what the Presentation of our Lord, is all about. What seems to be the case now is not as clear as it is when you shine some light on it. The light also opens the door to new possibilities that you had not seen without the light.

Think about the situation for these two venerable community pillars Simeon and Anna. We know that Simeon was chafing about the situation in Israel, about its status as a Roman colony (v. 25b). This despair must have affected Anna as well, though Luke does not say that. But we do know how devout she was, how despite being widowed she came daily to praise God (vv. 36-37).

Things do not look good in America today. Oh we may be a free country, not a colony. And yet are we not a nation in bondage to a racist past, captured by the mad quest for wealth and power which is dividing us along economic lines? Are many of us not in the distress that Anna must have felt as a widow? Widows in the ancient world had no resources and were totally dependent either on sons or a father (if living). Besides the grief, it was a precarious way to live. We've had a lot of grief and loss with the pandemic, and too many of us know the poverty which threatened Anna.

Certainly the baby Jesus did not seem an answer to Simeon's and Anna's prayers. How can this baby help us with the challenges of our personal lives and the big problems our nation faces? Martin Luther described the dilemma well in a sermon on this festival back in 1537. He put it this way:

> Simeon has a very penetrating eye. In this child there is not kingly men or royal garb to see, merely the form of a poor beggar... Simeon comes right up, without anyone's testimonial, and publicly attests: This *child* is the *Savior* of the world and a *light* to all the Gentiles... By reasoned judgment he would have had to say, "This is no king but a beggar-child." But he does not allow reason to judge by what his eyes behold...[2]

These reflections apply to you and me. How can Jesus solve America's problems, complex as they are? How can faith in Jesus make a difference in our personal lives when they are filled with despair or anxiety?

Well, the first matter to consider is that asking these questions illustrates our pride and arrogance. Unlike Simeon and Anna, we do not want to submit our reasoned judgment to faith. Because you and I trust our rational judgments and assessments more than we trust the insights of faith, of course we don't see how Jesus can solve these big problems. Luther again well expresses the situation:

> So now let everyone learn... the Lord God wants us to understand that *he* will not tolerate arrogance and that *he* puts down all who vaunt themselves, sparing only those that humble themselves. The world simply will not believe this and even today misuses simple and trifling gifts in arrogance.[3]

This is precisely what we have been doing with Jesus, since Christmas, as long as we have known him. We've not been looking to Jesus to shine light on things, not reveled like Simeon and Anna in what he is going to accomplish in our lives. No, we've been too arrogant, too trusting of our own resources for solving our problems, or just plain too discouraged to do anything about it.

I told you already that the Presentation of our Lord is a festival for penance. It is a time to confess our sin. Let's do it now. We have not really believed the promise and the hope Jesus brings.

Simeon and Anna told us differently, provided us with the right way to receive Jesus. Simeon even promised that Jesus would be not just a light to all the nations and glorify the Hebrews, why he'd be there to save the whole world (vv.30-32). And it's our fault, not God's or Jesus' fault. On the cross Jesus took all our arrogance, all our despair, and he put them to death! You might say his light burned them up. When all our arrogance is overcome, that's when America's going to work better, when all the things that divide us will wither away. When all the despair and sadnesses in our personal lives are burned up, life will look a whole lot better.

But these present realities have not gone away, you say. American problems are still with us. My grief, regrets, worries are still around, at least for a while. But that does not extinguish the light of Christ and the hope and new insight Jesus gives. Again, Martin Luther told us that. In another sermon, he remarked about how blind we are to Christ and his light:

> This is not to say, however, that all people will see the light or believe the *gospel*. The sun, indeed, shines its light into all the world, but many people go on sleeping; they are blind and do not see the light of the sun. It is not the sun's fault

that all people do not see the light of the sun, but their own fault, because they are either asleep or blind, or shade their windows and eyes, not wanting to see the sun's light.[4]

Yes, when you have light it gives you new insight into what is happening and where you are headed. Like Simeon sang about peace in his song about Jesus, the sight of our Lord gives you and me peace (v.29). The sight makes the future possible, gives you handles on the morass you feel like you are encountering. Shedding light on problems like you and I have makes dreams possible. And dreams are good things (especially the Christian dream). One poem by modern African-American poet Langston Hughes said it powerfully:

> Hold fast to dreams
> For if dreams die
> Life is a broken-winged bird
> That cannot fly.[5]

Nowhere to fly to if you do not have the Christian dream of Christ. Then you are stuck with the present American mess and your own personal problems. An earlier nineteenth-century English poet William Blake wrote a poem that seems directly related to our Bible lesson and today's festival. He wrote:

> Father, O Father! What do we hear,
> In this kind of unbelief and fear?
> The Land of Dreams is better far
> Above the light of the Morning Star.[6]

The Christian dream is a lot more real than the realities and the problems you and I are encountering. These problems all fade in face of what Jesus has done and is still doing with his light; their reality seems to fade away. Famed New Testaments scholar Rudolf Bultmann once put it this way:

> Eschatological [Christian Dream] preaching views the present time in light of the future and it says to men that this present world of nature and history, the world in which we live our lives and make our plans is not the only world, that this world is temporal and transitory, yes, ultimately empty and unreal in the face of eternity.[7]

What a good God we have, one who leads us away from the anxieties of the present! In the midst of this land of unbelief his light in Christ leads us to the land of dreams that is better, far better than even the morning star.

A theologian of the early church named Methodius preached a sermon on this text which ended with a song of praise that we can sing. It goes something like this:

> Hail to thee, thou Catholic Church, which has been planted in all the earth, and do thou rejoice with us... Hail, and rejoice, thou that wast once barren, and without seed unto godliness, but who hast now many children of faith...
>
> Hail thou treasure of the love of God... We together with thee sing our praises to Christ, Who has the power of life and earth... For *thou who* art incorruption hast come to set corruption free, that *thou* mightest render all things uncorrupt.[8]

Jesus came to earth to make all that is corrupt and painful in our lives no longer corrupt and painful, to shed his healing light and the Christian dream on all that's wrong in life.

NOTES

1. For this background on the festival, I am indebted to the insights of Luther Reed, *The Lutheran Liturgy* (Philadelphia: Fortress Press, 1947), p.554.
2. Martin Luther, "The Day of Mary's Purification" (1537), *The Complete Sermons of Martin Luther*, Vol.7, ed. John N. Lenker (Grand Rapids, MI: Baker, 2000), p.278.
3. Martin Luther, "The Day of the Purification of Mary" (1534), *The Complete Sermons of Martin Luther*, Vol.5, ed. John N. Lenker (Grand Rapids, MI: Baker, 2000), p.301.
4. Luther, "The Day of Mary's Purification," p.279.
5. Langston Hughes, "Dreams" (1922).
6. William Blake, "The Land of Dreams" (1800).
7. Rudolf Bultmann, *Jesus Christ and Mythology* (New York: Charles Scribner's Sons, 1958), p.23.
8. Methodius, "Oration Concerning Simeon and Anna" (n.d.), in *Anet-Nicene Fathers*, Vol.6, eds. Alexander Roberts and James Donaldson (2nd print; Peabody, MA: Hendrickson, 1995), pp.392-393.

Nobody Gets In A Rut With God: He's Always Got Us Moving On!

The little town of Capernaum was buzzing. News about the stranger and what he had done on the sabbath was spreading all over town. First Jesus had gone to the local synagogue to preach and discuss the Bible with the rabbis. His knowledge of scripture and the authority with which he taught amazed everyone (vv.21-22)! And on top of that he healed or at least quieted down a crazy man (vv.23-26). People heard the story and were bragging about him (v.28).

But that was not all that Jesus did on this sabbath. He left the synagogue entering the house of Simon Peter and Andrew along with James and John. Before long, Jesus learned Simon's mother-in-law was sick. (Apparently, according to Mark, Peter was from Capernaum.) Peter may have been hinting to Jesus about his performing a possible healing (vv.29-30). And before anyone in the house knew what had happened, Jesus had gone to the mother-in-law's bedside and lifted her up. Her fever was broken, and next thing Peter's mother-in-law was up and about taking care of everyone's needs (v.31)!

In a town the size of Capernaum, you just could not keep news like this quiet. By evening there was a whole flock of people just outside of Peter's door hoping Jesus would heal them too. And sure enough, he did (vv.32-34)!

By now Jesus had it made in Capernaum; he could have been elected king if he had wanted the title. And it is quite likely that this kind of praise and acclaim was something Jesus was not really used to and something we might expect him to enjoy. (We must concede that God welcomes praise.) After all, here was a poor carpenter's son who had known nothing but poverty his entire earthly life, and now suddenly he was enjoying all the fame and attention anyone could possible want.

Mark reported that the next day Jesus went out to a lonely place, a mile or so from town to pray. And after a while Peter and some of the other disciples found him. "Everyone's searching for you," Peter said, as if to hint that Jesus really ought to come back to town and enjoy all the attention he was getting (vv.35-37). And why not? After all, Jesus really did have it made back in Capernaum. On top of that, things were kind of nice for his followers back there too. It was probably quite nice for Peter and the other disciples to be "big shots." But then Jesus dropped the big bombshell on all of them. "Let us go on to the neighboring towns, so that I may proclaim the message there also; for that is what I came out to do." (v.38) Jesus was actually willing to give up all the acclaim, all the notoriety, to go out and try something new. And that's exactly what he did (v.39).

What does all this have to do with us? Can Jesus' decision to leave Capernaum in favor of going to preach in other cities and towns possibly be relevant to us in the decisions we make? That pretty much depends on what you understand is involved in a decision. From where I sit, a great number of the decisions we make involve a choice between doing things the way we've always done them or changing things. It comes down either to sticking with the way things are or seeking better outcomes by doing something creative and new.

Let me clarify this line of thinking by returning to our Bible story. You see, Jesus had spent some time in Capernaum, and as I've already noted, things were pretty comfortable. There was every reason to stay there, and seemingly very little reason to move on. But Jesus did move on.

Now I think a very good question to ask here would be why. Who in their right mind would leave a situation where they were well-known, respected, in short comfortable, for who knows what? I certainly would not want to do so, would you? But you know that Jesus of ours. He was a man of action who was rarely content to sit around accepting the way things were.

Think about this matter yourself for a moment. When thinking about Jesus, don't you almost always conceive of him as on the go? From one miracle to another, from one crowd to another, from one town to another. Always preaching, or teaching, or healing. In fact, if you note in today's lesson it starts with a reference to something happening "as soon as" Jesus left the synagogue (v. 29). According to Mark, Jesus was always doing things *immediately* (vv. 31, 42; 2:12; 5:2; 10:52).

Jesus' activity also tells us something about the way God operates. Because God is also someone on the go, never content with the way things are in our fallen world. The very act of creation itself represents a change on God's part from the way things were prior to creation. God's decision to send his Son to earth to die was a change from the way God was relating to us before he sent Jesus. Because God, you see, is always willing to change in order to make things better. Modern process theologians like John Cobb have spoken of God and his love as reflecting "creative transformation."[1]

All this means that God is oftentimes calling us to change, to do something new. There are great examples in the history of Christianity that demonstrate this point. Abram was perfectly happy living in the land of Haran, but God told him to leave there and follow him (Genesis 12). Slavery wasn't any bowl of cherries, but at least the ancient Hebrews knew what to expect. Yet they followed Moses into the wilderness, because they knew that that was God's will for them (Exodus 1:8-14; 12:33ff.). Likewise, the disciples, men like Peter, seemed perfectly content being fishermen until one day Jesus appeared and told them to give up what they had and to follow him (Mark 1:16-17). It's God's style: Get out of the rut and start moving on.

Change can be a good thing. Changes here in church, in your personal life, can be God's will. Not all changes are good, but those which are in accord with God's word are. In those cases, an unwillingness to change is kind of like asking Jesus to stay in Capernaum, to get in the way of spreading the gospel like he did. It would be a bit like Abraham saying to God, "No thank you, sir. I know it's a good offer you're making me if I'll just follow you, but I really don't want to leave my home here in Haran." Think of the millions who have known Abraham, Jew and Gentile. But I don't know anyone else from ancient Haran. How about you?

God often calls us to change. We have already seen today that that message is all over the Bible. This is not change for change sake or change which distorts the Bible. But because we don't live in a perfect world, for instead it's a world filled with flaws, a world where to keep things the way they are is to settle for the imperfect.

Just the same, we all know that change is hard. Former Metallica (now Megadeath) singer David Mustaine had it right when he purportedly once said: "Moving on is a simple thing, what it leaves behind is hard." No, change is hard in church. We grieve over what we have lost, since it's been that way so long that our congregation's pretty much the same as it was in our parents' and grandparents' time. But in light of the declining fortunes of American Christianity, the marked growth of the religiously unaffiliated, the American church has to change, not the word of God, but how we do business, community, how we worship, and definitely how we present ourselves! We're going to need to present ourselves less as "goodie-two-shoes" and conformists, but as rebels offering a lifestyle that is counter-cultural.

Yet it's not just here in church where we need change. This morning's gospel lesson also applies to our own lives as individuals. So many of us, even some of us right here, get locked into situations which have led to unhappiness, and yet we feel unable to change. Maybe it's an uncomfortable family situation or unsatisfying work. Oprah Winfrey was on the money when she claimed, "You can't keep blaming somebody else for your dysfunction. Life really is about moving on."

Let's get real about life as we are living it every day, without reference to eternity. From that standpoint, life is pretty empty and meaningless, just a cycle of births, sicknesses, and death. We've got to break that cycle, to get out of the rut we're in. But we can't, not on our own. There's a Baptist preacher, Matt Eachus, with a quote on the internet that says it all. He wrote: "When we wrap our minds and hearts around God's gracious work in the gospel and root ourselves in Jesus, we find the strength and power to change, because the power to change comes from him alone."

Followers of Jesus, Christians, are people out to change things, to move on and rebel against all the meaninglessness of their present situation. It is as the famed twentieth-century champion against fundamentalism Harry Emerson Fosdick once put it: "Christians are supposed not merely to endure change, not even to profit by it, but to cause it." What else is repentance that we Christians stress, but change. In his famous Ninety-Five Theses, Martin Luther said the whole of Christian life is daily repentance. As he put it, "When our Lord and Master Jesus Christ said, ``Repent'' (Matthew 4:17), he willed the entire life of believers to be one of repentance." In other words, every day Christians are changing, always moving on like Jesus did.

This lifestyle of always being ready to move on, a discontent with the status quo and the rut we're in, is a truly counter-cultural, rebellious way of life. This kind of rebellious lifestyle is most reminiscent of the way of life French Existentialist Philosopher Albert Camus urged us to live. Rebellion he [and Jesus] tells us is the refusal to let the world be what it is, to assert meaning in face of the uncompromising meaninglessness of ordinary life. The rebel [the Christian] moves on from what is for the sake that is more than himself.[2] Think for yourself if this style of life is not what the millennials and others who have left the church are looking for in life. A church committed to this style of life can turn things around. And the wonder of it all is that in Jesus God is working on us to change. No two ways about it: our Lord Jesus won't let this church, you, or me get stuck in the mud and its rut. He's committed to get us moving on!

NOTES
1. John B. Cobb and David Ray Griffin, *Process Theology: an Introductory Exposition* (Philadelphia: Westminster, 1976), p.100.
2. Albert Camus, *The Rebel*, trans. Anthony Bower (New York: Vintage Books, 1956), pp. 10-11,14-15,306.

Transfiguration Sunday
Mark 9:2-9

Christ Glorified: The End Has Come!

The Transfiguration: It's a great story. But what does it matter in everyday twenty-first-century life? Let's see.

Jesus had told his followers of his coming death and resurrection, just in the previous week (8:31 — 9:2a). Six days later Jesus took with him Peter, James, and John, leading all of them to the top of a high mountain. And right before their eyes he was transfigured before them (v.h2). His clothes became dazzlingly white (v.h3)! Then Moses and Elijah appeared among them (v.h4). (There was a tradition that both Moses and Elijah had been translated directly into heavenly life [Deuteronomy 34:5-6; 2 Kings 2:9-12].) Imagine the fright of the disciples, the sheer terror they felt (v. 6). No surprise then that not knowing what to say Peter asks Jesus if he and his compatriots should make different tents (the usual dwelling places of divine beings in ancient Israel [Exodus 25:1-9]) for Jesus, Moses, and Elijah (v.5).

Then a cloud overshadowed them all. Encounters with God in the Old Testament often included a cloud (Exodus 24:15-18; Ezekiel 1:4). And a voice was heard: "This is my Son, the beloved. Listen to him." (vv.7-8). Silence followed. Jesus stood alone (v.8). And then he told his followers to say nothing about what had happened until he had risen from the dead (v.9).

Yes, it's a great story: But that question remains: What does the Transfiguration have to say to us?

Jesus himself answered this question in part. The Transfiguration has to do with Easter, with the resurrection. That is why Jesus wanted to keep things quiet about this miracle until he had risen (v.9). Just as Easter is about our own resurrection (1 Corinthians 15:12), so Easter and in turn the Transfiguration are signs of the end. The story of today's miracle gets you and me looking to the future, to eternity. How appropriate that in concluding this sequence of the Bible's great stories we be directed to start looking to the end of time, the end of all historical stories.

How does this connection between the miracle we commemorate today and Easter and eternity impact every-day Monday through Saturday living? Mark's version of the Transfiguration story gives us some clues. Typical of Mark, the account of this event portrays the disciples as messed up in their understanding of what they had seen. They were afraid, Mark said (vv.5-6). Isn't that the way it is with you and me? We are pathetically unmoved by this great account that it no longer or never thrills us. Come clean, friends. The Transfiguration is not making much of a difference in your everyday life.

Oh, but our sin is not the last word when it comes to the Transfiguration. It is also a story about Jesus' conquest at Easter and how he conquers our sin. Hear the words of Martin Luther on the subject:

> This appearance teaches us also that we should despise death, and look upon it merely as an emigration or a sleep. In short, this appearance proves that this life is nothing at all in comparison with the future life.

Fourthly, this appearance proves that *sin is overcome.* For it necessarily follows as an incontrovertible conclusion, that, where death is overcome, there sin is also overcome.[1]

The Transfiguration reminds us that despite our lack of faith and excitement about Jesus, sin does not have a chance! Neither does death. The realities of the future, the end, the resurrection, are already in sight.

The Reformer John Calvin offered an intriguing way of explaining how the story of the Transfiguration makes clear that we are in a new era at the end of time. His comments also remind us of the appearance of Moses and Elijah at the event. Calvin says they came "to wait upon Christ."[2] The famed reformer then proceeds with the comment:

> But why did these two [Moses and Elijah] appear, rather than others who equally belonged to the company of the holy fathers? It was intended to demonstrate that Christ alone is the end of the *law* and of the *prophets*...[3]

This makes it clear that the Transfiguration is a testimony that Christ makes the law and the demand to do good works in order to be saved, has been subordinated to himself. The miracle and Christ's glorification makes it clear that God will no longer judge us by our works. The end time of God's will to save without works of the law has now come. The Transfiguration is a testimony that the end of the law has come, the old era is waning. God's love overcomes.

This new era of God's love prevailing over everything is also nicely articulated by Calvin. We note the way in which Christ's clothes were transformed into a dazzling whiteness (v.3). This whiteness was dazzling, as was his appearance at the Transfiguration. So dazzling, John Calvin wrote, that it can't help but change you. He wrote:

> But when the secret grace of God quickens it, all the senses must be affected in such a manner that men will be prepared to follow wherever God calls them.[4]

You don't leave a miracle unchanged; you can't keep on going like everything is the same. The power of God's grace, when you see the glory of the Transfiguration won't let you go. It will be working on you this week, prodding you to look at life from an end time point of view.

Yes the glorified Christ, the transfigured and risen Jesus will be watching you all week. He'll be keeping his eye on you and me, not as a judge but as a lover. How can a knowledge of that sort of love and forgiveness not change you? Captivated by a love like that we're likely to start singing a song once taught by the famed Irish playwright and political activist George Bernard Shaw:

> You are my inspiration and my folly. You are my light across the sea, my million nameless joys, and my day's wage. You are my divinity, my madness, my selfishness, my transfiguration and purification. You are my rapscallionly fellow vagabond, my tempter and star. I want you.

Basking in a love like that, how can you and I not want to change the world, have God use us to bring in a new era when everyone we meet can be loved like this and love others that way? What difference does the Transfiguration make? It gives us a vision of our beloved Jesus so alluring that you and I will never be the same once we've really uncovered our eyes and beheld that love in all its glory. To paraphrase Shaw, Christ is now our light across the sea, our madness, tempter, and star. We can't help but want him. So mesmerizing this divine love for you and me is that all you'll feel is a burning desire to want to give it back. And isn't that what heaven is all about? The Transfiguration is a great story to launch you into the rest and the end of your life!

NOTES

1. Martin Luther, "Notes On the Gospel" (n.d)
2. John Calvin, *Commentary On a Harmony of the Evangelists, Matthew, Mark, and Luke* (1553), in *Calvin's Commentaries*, Vol.XVI/2, trans. William Pringle (Grand Rapids, MI: Baker, 2005). p.310.
3. *Ibid.*, p.311.
4. *Ibid.*, Vol.XVII/2, p.74

www.ingramcontent.com/pod-product-compliance
Lightning Source LLC
LaVergne TN
LVHW091206080426
835509LV00006B/863